The Jan Braai Rules

1. Nothing beats a real wood fire.

2. Gas is Afrikaans for a guest at your braai, not something you braai with.

3. Braaing is the only fat-negative way of cooking food. Even when you steam food, the fat in it stays behind. When you braai, the fat drips out. Be healthy and braai your food.

4. Try never to braai with indigenous wood. Alien vegetation like Rooikrans and black wattle drink lots of groundwater so rather burn them. Besides, after all these sports world cups they've knocked us out of, it feels good to burn Australian rubbish.

5. Braaing is a direct form of energy use, from the coals to your meat. With conventional electricity there is a lot spillage between the power plant, power lines, electricity box, wires, stove and pan. If you love the earth, braai.

6. Have enough ice at your braai. Use it for your Klippies and coke, to keep beer cold, and to treat burn wounds with.

7. Smoke flies to pretty people, so have enough of them at your braai and there will be no smoke in your eyes.

8. Animals eat grass, leaves and vegetables all their lives and convert it to meat. Eating meat is like eating vitamin pills.

9. A cow must only be killed once. Do not braai you steak until the flavour is dead.

10. A *braaibroodjie* is your chance in life to have your bread buttered on both sides – use it.

Jan Braai
Fireworks

JanBraai *Fireworks*

BOOKSTORM

MACMILLAN

CONTENTS

HOW TO BRAAI THE PERFECT STEAK

To braai the perfect steak at your own home is one of those things you should be able to do with ease. As long as you stick to a few basic guidelines and pay attention to what you are doing, you will master this skill in no time. Once you can comfortably braai an awesome steak at home, this knowledge, skill and experience will be your foundation for doing it anywhere else, in whatever strange braaing conditions life might throw at you.

To braai the perfect steak, the actual steak that you are braaing has to be of a certain quality. However well you braai it, a bad piece of meat is never going to turn out great. Later on in this book we go into more detail about that but, first things first: the following foundational principles will equip you with a culture of excellent steak braaing that you can use for the rest of your life.

1. The steak should be at room temperature by the time it goes onto the fire.

- If it is in the fridge, take the steak out 20 minutes before you want to braai it, and leave it in the shade or indoors. (When you make the effort to buy great steaks, you are probably not going to freeze them, but if the steaks you want to braai are frozen, transfer them from the freezer to the fridge at least a day in advance to allow them to thaw slowly.)
- It's already 100% protein, so cover it with a cloth to keep the flies and bugs away. If there are dogs or hyenas around, place the steak well outside their reach.

2. You need plenty of extremely hot coals.

- If you are making a real fire with real wood, and this is the best way to braai, make a big fire from the outset. Do not make a medium-sized fire and add more wood later. By the time the second batch of wood has burnt out, the coals from the first batch will be half dead. Once the meat goes onto the fire, the process will be over quickly, so if you want to stand around the fire and discuss life with your guests for a few hours before you eat, make a medium-sized fire by all means. But when you intend to braai, add lots of wood, wait until it's burnt out, then braai.
- If the petrol station only had wet wood available and you have to use charcoal, light quite a lot of it. For a small braai, consider half a bag. It's not uncommon for me to use a whole bag of charcoal when braaing steaks for a dinner party.

- If you are wondering whether you have enough heat, then the answer is probably no. For these easy steps to a perfect steak to work, you need peace of mind that your coals are extremely hot. This is essential.

3. The exact height of your grid is not important. Anything between 5 and 15 centimetres is fine.

- When you braai steaks at your own home, always braai them on the same height and know exactly what that height is.
- When you are braaing at a new location, compare the height of the grid to the height of the grid at home, and adjust the braaing time accordingly.

4. Steaks should be done medium rare.

- If you really prefer your steaks rare and aren't just saying it to try and sound one up on everybody else ordering medium rare, then you shouldn't be ordering rare steaks anyway. There are two great dishes for you to try – Steak Tartare and Beef Carpaccio.
- If you prefer your steaks medium, then start buying superior quality steaks, learn how to braai them better, and acquire the taste of enjoying them medium rare.
- If you like your steaks medium well or well done, then why exactly are you reading this section of the book? You're probably quite capable of messing the meat up all by yourself.
- If one of your guests asks for medium, and you have prepared enough extremely hot coals to start with, then there will be quite

enough heat to get their steak medium by the time everybody else has sat down and been served. This should not happen too often, as most classy people nowadays are aware that steak should be enjoyed medium rare.

- If any of your guests wants their steak well done, refuse.

5. Add salt whenever you want to.

- I honestly don't think it makes much difference to meat tenderness or juiciness whether you add the salt before, during or after the braai.

6. Take note of the time when the steaks go onto the grid and take them off after about 7 minutes.

- Steaks cut to a thickness of 2.5 cm to 3 cm, braaied on extremely hot coals, and at a grid height of 10 cm, take about 7 minutes in total to become medium rare.
- Break up the 7 minutes as follows: After 2 minutes turn the steaks for the first time, then turn them again after another 2 minutes; with a final turn 1½ minutes later. Leave steaks on the fire for another 1½ minutes after which they will be perfect.
- It's perfectly acceptable to ask someone else to keep the time while you do the work.

7. Use braai tongs, not a fork, to turn the meat. A fork will make holes in the meat, and you might lose some juice.

8. The meat should be dry when it goes onto the fire; do not baste until both sides of the meat have been over the coals for 2 minutes each.

- As the heat from the coals seals the outside of the meat facing downwards, certain chemical reactions occur in the meat which develop part of the flavour. If you baste the meat before those chemical reactions have happened, the basting will boil and steam the side of the meat. Your steak will have less braai taste.

9. If you are using a hinged grid that closes (*toeklaprooster*) then obviously all the steaks will be turned at the same time. If you are turning the steaks one by one then turn them in the order that they went onto the grid and also remove them from the grid in that order.

10. Meat needs to 'rest' a bit after the braai, before you eat it.

- This lets the juices settle down and not all run out when you slice the meat.
- Watch out that the steak does not end up cold by the time you eat it. If you heat up the plates you will be eating from, this should not be a problem.
- By the time everyone has sat down and been served, the meat has rested enough.
- Do not put the steaks in an aluminium braai bowl with lots of other meat and then into an oven where they will steam for another hour while some fool is braaing his frozen chicken. Your steaks will be ruined.

ADJUSTMENTS

Once you have followed the above steps, you need to make an honest assessment of whether the steaks were perfect. If they were not, you need to repeat the steps, making slight adjustments until you have fine-tuned your technique to perfection. The most obvious adjustments to make are:

- If the steaks are burnt black on the outside, there is a very good chance that it's not the meat but the marinade or spices that are burnt. The easiest way to get rid of this problem is not to marinate the meat in future.
- If the steaks are done medium or well, then they were probably cut too thin. In future, braai steaks that are thicker, or braai the same steaks but for a shorter time.
- If the steaks look perfect but are quite tough or tasteless, buy your steaks from a different place in future.
- If the steaks are underdone, then your fire was not hot enough. Repeat the process, and really go all out with that fire next time. You'll be surprised how much heat a piece of unmarinated meat can withstand for 7 minutes without getting burnt. Alternatively, your steaks are very thick; in that case, increase your braai time slightly.

Once you can braai steaks perfectly at home, you can easily do it anywhere else as well. If there are less-than-ideal coals, try to set the grid very low. If the steaks are cut exceptionally thick, braai them for longer, and vice versa if they are cut especially thin. If the grid only has one setting and that is very high, allow a little extra braaing time.

NOW, BEFORE YOU START …

At this stage you probably have no idea whether you will actually enjoy reading this book or if you will find the information within it useful. As such you probably don't really care who helped me to make it a success, as you don't even know whether you consider it a success. So, right at the end of this book, after the chapter called 'What is a Man-Oven?' is a section entitled 'Acknowledgements'. By the time you get there, you'll know if you want to read it.

This book is about braaing, about making fires with wood and about you confidently cooking great meals on the coals of that fire. Due to the unique direction my life has taken over the past few years, I've been fortunate enough to braai quite often, with diverse people, in various beautiful places, using different techniques. As a result, there is now quite a bit of tacit knowledge in my head that I want to share with you – just to bring you up to speed, so to speak. To be able to harvest all the knowledge in this book properly, you will need to read it from cover to cover at first as that is the way I have written it and mean it to be read. You can then skip directly to specific recipes on future occasions. The nature of tacit knowledge is such that one is not always aware of all one knows, and some things might be quite important but only mentioned once. In those cases where you pick up a tip that is relevant to all other braais, generalise it and apply it to your other braai recipes, even if I do not mention it in each of them.

On the topic of braaing, I'm probably the most interviewed person in South Africa and consequently a good judge of what people want to know when it comes to braaing. I have addressed all of those questions somewhere in this book. *Fireworks* contains a considerable mass of information generously spiced with a large dose of personal prejudice.

I'm quite opinionated in this book, and for the times when this offends you I apologise in advance. My aim was to write a book that will add value to your life, and to write it in such a way that it will be useful and useable. If you've never braaied a specific cut of meat before, I believe that giving you a book with vague statements like 'braai it to your liking' makes no sense whatsoever. How can you know what you like if you've never done it before? For example then, I will tell you to braai something for exactly 10 minutes because that's how I do it to get the result that I think tastes best. Should your taste be different, braai it for 8 or 12 minutes next time – but you've already taken a step forward in your braaing knowledge and skills, which means I've achieved my objective.

This book is not about National Braai Day. I'm too young for that and National Braai Day is too young for that. But what I will say is that in National Braai Day, we South Africans have a realistic opportunity to entrench and cement a national day of celebration for our country, within our lifetimes. I believe that having a national day of celebration could play a significant role in nation-building and social cohesion as the observance of our shared heritage can truly bind us together. In Africa, a fire is the traditional place of gathering. I urge you to get together with your friends and family around a fire on 24 September every year to celebrate our heritage, share stories and pass on traditions. Help me spread that word!

Jan Braai

OTHER IMPORTANT THINGS YOU NEED TO KNOW

DISCLAIMER

At the time of writing, I believed the things written in this book to be correct. Having said that, some of the statements I make are written like fact, when they are clearly opinion. So when you read things that I say and you don't agree with them, that's all there is to it - I gave my opinion, and you disagreed.

Let's test this principle right away and find out whether you find the above paragraph upsetting or whether you can live with it. I truly believe every braaier should have a digital instant-read meat thermometer. Turn to page 16 to find out why. And now, whether you agree or not, go and buy yourself one.

Lastly, unless otherwise stated, all human characters appearing in this work are fictitious. Any resemblance to real persons, living or dead, is purely coincidental. On the other hand, all animals appearing in this book, living or dead, but more often dead, are real. Any reference to a particular animal is exactly that, a reference to that animal.

THE HISTORY OF BRAAING IN SOUTH AFRICA

Scientifically speaking, South Africans are not only the best braaiers in the world, but braaing also originated here. During the recording of the first Jan Braai TV show in 2011, we visited the Swartkrans excavation site, which forms part of the fossil site at the Cradle of Humankind. As you probably know, this is one of South Africa's eight UNESCO World Heritage Sites. I toured the site together with the pioneering scientist Dr Bob Brain (real name). Dr Brain found conclusive proof that early humans controlled fire for over 1 million years. Our command of fire, which is also called 'pyrotechnology', is distinctive to hominids (our direct ancestors) and represents a major turning point in human evolution. It basically transformed us from prey to predator.

The theory is that the first braais happened when meat was accidentally dropped into fires, later removed and then eaten. The early humans found that the cooked meat not only tasted better than raw meat, but could also be chewed more easily. The rest is history, as they started dropping meat on and into fires on a regular basis. An additional advantage of their control of fire was that they were able to ward off predators. The early humans also crafted stone tools like axes and cleavers. Their control of fire meant that they could leave Africa and travel into the northern hemisphere and survive in the cold.

The scientists have proved that the early humans who were living in the area were definitely responsible for controlling fire. A sharp reader like you might ask: How do you know the fires weren't just accidental bush fires started by lightning? To answer this, Dr Brain tested the charred remains of the bones that were excavated. He found that the ferocity of the burn that created the charred remains was much higher than any heat produced by bush fires, so it had to have been done by a fire that was repeatedly fed with wood.

It is very fitting then, I think you will agree, that South Africa has a National Braai Day to celebrate this important part of our heritage.

JUICINESS, TENDERNESS AND FLAVOUR

The pleasure of eating braaied meat is directly related to three features of the meat: juiciness, tenderness and flavour.

Juiciness depends mainly on the end temperature of your meat. This means that the more 'done' you braai your meat, the drier it will be. Essentially you need to braai meat to exactly the point at which it is ready for consumption and no more. In this book we've tested that point to be at internal temperatures of 55–57°C for beef, 60–63°C for lamb, 71°C for pork and 77°C for chicken. The second factor that influences the juiciness of meat is the amount of fat that it contains, hence the constant talk about 'marbled' meat.

When it comes to tenderness, the most important driver is the location of the muscle on the animal. Basically, the more exercise a muscle did during an animal's life, the less tender it will be, and vice versa. That is, for example, why fillet steak is consistently a very tender cut and brisket is a fairly tough cut of meat. The age of an animal also plays a role and meat from younger animals is more tender than meat from older animals – that's why we prefer lamb to mutton. Furthermore, the ageing of meat plays a vitally important role in its tenderness as enzymes break down the proteins in the meat during the ageing process. In short, aged meat will be more tender than non-aged meat. Marinating meat and giving it a few tenderising hits with your meat mallet are popular ways to make the meat you've already bought more tender. Lastly, the longer you braai meat, the more liquid it loses and the more liquid it loses, the tougher it becomes, which is another reason not to overbraai your meat.

Braaied meat gets its characteristic flavour from the process of braaing. Once the surface temperature of the meat goes past 154°C there is a chemical reaction between some of the proteins and sugars in the meat, which scientists call the Milliard reaction. This reaction gives the surface of the meat that brown colour, crunchy texture and unique flavour. (Don't confuse this brown colour with the black colour of burnt food; that's something different.) The flavour generated during the Milliard reaction, along with smoke from the fire and coals, gives braaied meat its typical taste. As you know water boils at 100°C and that is why, although you can cook meat in this way, boiled or steamed meat will never taste the same as braaied meat. The marinades, spices and sauces that you use on your meat is the other big factor determining taste, but that is a topic we deal with extensively in the rest of this book.

BRAAING TIMES ARE RELATIVE SO BUY A MEAT THERMOMETER

In many of the recipes in this book I suggest braaing times for certain cuts of meat. These are all guidelines and are supposed to give you a general feel for when to check whether the meat is ready. Braaing times can and will fluctuate.

Factors that may influence braaing times include:

- meat thickness and size
- amount of meat on the grid
- size of the fire
- type of wood used
- length of time you waited to start braaing after the fire burnt out
- wind speed and direction
- air temperature
- height of the grid
- material your braai place is made of (a brick fireplace will retain more heat from the fire than a thin layer of steel, for instance)

Assuming you usually braai at your own home and under the same conditions, I believe that by timing your braais and adjusting the braai time for changing circumstances like the ones mentioned above, in time you can develop a feel for, and make a fairly good estimate of, when meat will be ready by looking at the time; this is especially true for meats like steak, lamb chops and boerewors.

Poking meat with your finger and comparing its resilience or hardness to one of your body parts in order to judge whether it is done is silly. Factors that may influence the resilience of a person's body parts include whether you are:

- fit or unfit
- fat or thin
- young or old.

Factors that may influence the resilience of a piece of meat on the braai include:

- the cut of meat (e.g. fillet vs rump)
- the age of animal when slaughtered (e.g lamb vs mutton)
- the size of the meat (big pieces can be softer)
- how long the meat was aged (aged is softer than fresh).

Professional chefs poke hundreds of steaks per day and all those steaks come from the same supplier and were aged in the same way so they should know what the steaks they cook in their restaurant feel like when they are ready. I, on the other hand, struggle. It should be evident that I feel pretty strongly about this thermometer topic by virtue of the fact that an entire page of this book is dedicated to the subject.

The thermometer that you want is called a 'digital instant-read thermometer' and at the time of writing this book they had a price tag roughly equal to 1 kg of sirloin steak, so buying one should be a no-brainer. To braai a whole chicken, butterflied leg of lamb or any other thick piece of meat without one and risk serving it raw or overcooked and dry simply does not make sense. If you just save 1 kg of quality meat by using your meat thermometer, it already paid for itself. Simplify your life and get one, and whenever you are unsure about whether the meat is ready, as happens so often with difficult meats like pork and chicken or any thick piece of meat, simply stick the thermometer into the thickest part of the meat and check whether it's done.

RECOMMENDED INTERNAL TEMPERATURE FOR MEAT

	Degrees Celsius (°C) in thickest part	Doneness
beef	55–57	medium rare
lamb	60–63	medium rare
pork	71	medium
chicken	77	done

MEASUREMENTS IN THIS BOOK

The nature of a braai recipe is that it is pretty unscientific and imprecise. If you add a little more garlic, salt or chilli the meal will taste more strongly of that ingredient and if you add less, the taste will be weaker. Use your common sense.

That said you'll make life easier for yourself by investing in three measurement tools: a cup (250 ml), a tot glass (25 ml) and a teaspoon (5 ml). Teaspoon is abbreviated to tsp. Calibrate them by using water to check that 5 teaspoons go into a tot and that 10 tots go into a cup. When the measuring cup, tot glass or measuring teaspoon is full but flat as it is when you fill it with liquid, it contains the given volume. When the recipe calls for half a cup or half a tot don't panic, just fill the cup or glass halfway; it's as easy as that.

SAFETY ISSUES

Braaied well, your meat should taste excellent but you don't want to taste it twice. Be sure to keep to some basic safety rules when preparing your meals for the sake of your and your guests' health.

- Wash your hands well before you start preparing and handling the food. If you take a break, wash them again before you touch anything you're going to serve up.
- Keep meat that is marinating in a cool place or fridge so that the heat of the day doesn't cause it to go off.
- Don't use marinade with raw meat juices in it as a sauce – either boil it first and then use as a sauce on the braaied meat or paint it onto the meat before the last 5 minutes of braaing time so it has a chance to cook too.

THE ULTIMATE BRAAI KIT

At a bare minimum you need a braai grid and something to rest it on, but my braai kit consists of:

1. **Two identical *toeklaproosters*** or grids with a hinged lid that can be closed. Sometimes not everything you want to braai fits onto one grid and at other times you want to load one grid while the other one is still on the fire. They need to be the same size so that you can braai your *braaibroodjies* in one right on top of your meat in the other. In emergencies I do buy normal steel grids but I think the extra money you pay for stainless steel grids is worth it. I prefer the grids that are not held together with rings at the top but that you can take apart completely and choose the level at which to insert the other half of the grid.

2. **One flat grid** with thicker rods for braaing items like *roosterkoek* and patties that tend to 'sink' into a normal grid and get stuck.

3. **A cast-iron pot** for making *potjie* and performing various other tasks. You can completely justify having a few pots of different shapes and sizes. For more on this topic go to page 140.

4. **A steel, fireproof pan** for doing the types of things you do in a pan, but on a fire. Like making *Bratkartoffeln* (page 160).

5. **A braai pan with holes** or a basket made from mesh wire to braai prawns, vegetables or any other small items that will fall through a grid. Much easier than always having to put them on skewers.

6. **At least three pairs of proper braai tongs** – one for the fire, one for raw meat and one for braaied meat. At home I have about 20 pairs of identical tongs so if I'm braaing meat, fish and vegetables for fussy guests I can use different tongs to handle the different types of food. I throw all the used tongs into the dishwasher after the braai so that they are always clean and shiny, ready for my next braai.

7. **Six bricks**. These are usually available at the building site nearest to your house. The bricks are to balance the grid on. With six bricks you can achieve a phenomenal number of different height settings, more than you will ever need. You can also use a line of bricks as a border to keep coals and heat in a certain area of the braai as needed.

8. **Two sturdy triangles** of different heights to rest your grid on, for when you can't find your bricks. They are also convenient when you want to seal meat on high heat and then lift it to a more gentle heat for the remainder of the cooking time. Alternatively, when the coals are very hot to begin with you can start on the high triangle and then use the lower one as the heat of the coals dies down.

9. **One pair of leather welding gloves**. Sometimes one or all of your fire, grid, tongs, bricks, triangles and *potjie* just get too hot to control with bare hands. It's better to have gloves on standby than to let the meat burn while you think of a way to touch that grid.

10. **One water pistol**. There is absolutely no better way to keep control and enforce discipline on flare-ups and fires that want to burn your food.

11. **Two cutting boards** – one for raw meat and one for braaied meat.

12. **A headlamp**, for night-time braaing. Remember not to look other people in the eye while your headlamp is on full power.

13. At least **one proper chef's knife**, preferably more. You can never have too many knives. You might as well get a good carving knife and fork set as well.

14. **A knife sharpener**. Blunt knives are like wet wood.

15. **One braai bowl**. They are usually sold with a lid that can double up as your second braai bowl. In general I'm very much against closing meat in a braai bowl and then letting it steam on low heat while you braai other things. This spoils the crisp sides of meat and also frequently overcooks it. Plan your braai better and have everything ready at the same time.

16. **Non-reactive bowls** for marinating meat. These can be glass, plastic or stainless steel and should have lids. We will call them marinating bowls in the recipes.

17. **A pestle and mortar** to crush herbs and spices.

18. **A digital instant-read meat thermometer**. This is the 21st century so get one. More on this topic on page 16.

19. **A steel wire brush** to clean the grid after you have heated it on the fire.

20. **A basting brush** for painting marinade onto the meat.

21. **A watch** for checking how long the meat is on the fire. Dry, overbraaied food is not fun; just get into the habit of checking how long the meat has been cooking for and taking it off when is it ready.

STOCK YOUR BRAAI PANTRY

To make the recipes in this book exactly you clearly need all the ingredients but generally I don't think it's worth a trip to the supermarket to go and get a single ingredient. Just leave it out, or use something that tastes similar. If the ingredient is crucial to the dish, you obviously need it. You can't braai steak without steak.

You will notice that most, if not all, the ingredients in the recipes are widely available in South Africa. Apart from the fresh ingredients, I suggest you build up a collection of sauces, spices and herbs that you need on a frequent basis when you braai. You need less than you might think to create a wide range of dishes. It's simply the quantities and braai techniques that differ.

I counted the number of times each ingredient appears in this book. Logically then, in order of importance, these are the things I think you should stock in your braai kitchen on a permanent basis. All recipes understandably have other ingredients as well, including meat, but keeping these items in your kitchen will save you many unnecessary trips to the supermarket. Start off by buying the top 20, all the way down to white wine (this is a coincidence) and then acquire the rest as you need them for specific recipes.

	Ingredient	Times mentioned
1	salt	60
2	pepper	43
3	garlic	40
4	olive oil	37
5	lemon juice[1]	25
6	butter	23
7	parsley	19
8	onion	18
9	chilli[2]	14
10	fresh cream	14
11	vinegar[3]	14
12	oregano	11
13	paprika[4]	11
14	ginger	9
15	mustard[5]	9
16	honey	8
17	sugar	7
18	soy sauce	6

	Ingredient	Times mentioned
19	thyme	6
20	white wine[6]	6
21	coriander	5
22	rosemary	5
23	tomato paste	5
24	bay leaves	4
25	masala	4
26	plain yoghurt	4
27	sherry/port	4
28	turmeric	4
29	apricot jam	3
30	brandy[7]	3
31	chutney	3
32	curry	3
33	tomato sauce	3
34	Worcestershire sauce	3
35	apple juice	2
36	basil	2

	Ingredient	Times mentioned
37	cumin	2
38	almond	1
39	cinnamon	1
40	mint	1
41	rocket	1
42	sage	1

1 fresh or from the green bottle with the yellow cap
2 powder, flakes and fresh (I find chilli powder is the most consistent and reliable way to add burn to a dish but you need to have at least the African Bird's Eye chilli in your herb garden)
3 brown, red, white, grape (I rarely use balsamic) – buy the whole lot or just one and use it for everything
4 powder – fresh green, yellow and red peppers not included here
5 includes Dijon and Hot English mustard powder
6 number of times used as an ingredient, but this is clearly much more important than that
7 obviously present at all your braais – this is just the number of times it's used as an ingredient

HERB GARDEN

I consider a herb garden with the following plants to be decent but not extreme: parsley, oregano, thyme, rosemary, sage, basil, mint, rocket, chilli, a bay tree and two lemon trees. This is the extent of my herb garden at home and I encourage you to cultivate a similar one at your home.

Beef

Otherwise known as steak

There are a lot of politics in the cattle industry. So much so that I'm starting this page with a little disclaimer: Nothing on this page should be read as fact. These are my personal opinions at the time of writing the book and where sentences look like statements or fact, they are my current understanding of a certain concept, relayed in layman's terms.

GRASS-FED AND GRAIN-FED BEEF

- Grass and grain both grow in fields. In the context of food for cattle, the grass grows wild and the grain is cultivated.
- Grass-fed beef refers to the meat from cattle that roamed and grazed relatively freely in fields where, among other things, grass was growing. Grass-fed beef could be but is not necessarily free-range beef.
- Grain-fed beef refers to the meat from cattle that lived in a feedlot and were fed grain. As per the definition, grain-fed beef can never be free range as the animals were living in confinement and were fed as opposed to being able to graze for food.

WHICH IS BETTER?

- As grass-fed animals have to walk around and graze in a field, they do more exercise than their grain-fed counterparts and generally take a bit longer to reach market weight. Grass-fed meat can thus be tougher yet more tasty.
- As grain-fed animals live in close confinement, they possibly have more stress, which could lead to tougher meat. But they are probably more tender from doing less exercise to get their food.
- Grass-fed animals theoretically eat what cattle were naturally supposed to eat.
- Grain-fed animals eat a controlled diet of grain. You know what you get, but they possibly also need more medicine and supplements due to their confined living conditions.
- When offered both for the same price, I'd go for the grass-fed. But this is rarely the case so what usually determines my buying decision is how the meat was aged.

DRY-AGED AND WET-AGED STEAK

- Wet-aged means that the steak was vacuum-packed for most of its ageing time. There was no mass loss as the juices and blood that were in the steak at the time of vacuum-packing are still in there.
- Dry-aged means that the steak is from a piece of meat that hung in a cold room at about 2°C for most of its ageing time. During this time there was significant mass loss as the meat slowly started to dry out. There is additional overall mass loss with dry-aged meat as the outsides of the big piece of meat that is aged dries out completely and needs to be discarded at the end of the ageing process. You cannot dry-age single portions of meat. Whole big pieces need to be aged on the bone and then separated into portions when you want to consume them.

WHICH IS BETTER?

I'm of the opinion that dry-aged is superior to wet-aged meat. As moisture goes out of the meat, flavour is left behind and the result is a more concentrated and richly flavoured steak. Moisture will also go out of a wet-aged steak, but under circumstances where it takes flavour with it (all those juices and blood left in the packaging when you cut it open). My perception is also that dry-aged steak is more tender. As the mass loss can be about 20% during the ageing process, you must be prepared to pay more for dry-aged than wet-aged steak. Think about it: 1 kg of dry-aged meat is actually the same as 1.2 kg of wet-aged meat. In addition, the butcher needs a special fridge for dry-ageing and the process requires more labour and attention.

As hanging large pieces of meat is not practical for the big supermarket chains, I suggest a compromise where premium meat is hung for a while and then cut into individual portions, vacuum packed and distributed.

CAPE TOWN

RUMP STEAK WITH GARLIC BUTTER

Steak is a unique animal that needs to be braaied on extremely hot coals to sear the outside while keeping the inside medium rare and juicy. This poses a problem when you're braaing a variety of meat, as the steak needs to go on first when the coals are still in a furious state of heat. By the time everything else is braaied the steak will be completely cold, or worse, someone might have put it in a covered bowl and steamed it on low heat until it became a grey and soggy piece of rubber.

At big braais I sometimes solve this problem by braaing the steaks at the perfect time, just after the fire has burned out and the coals are at their hottest, and then serving them as a starter.

WHAT YOU NEED (per person)
50-100 g steak (this is a snack)
salt and pepper
1 roll or tube of garlic butter (yes, you're allowed to buy those ready-made rolls at the shop)

WHAT TO DO

1. Make a very hot fire.

2. Take the steak out the fridge and bring it to room temperature 20 minutes before the braai. If there's a lot of blood or juice in the packaging when you remove the steak, wash the meat under cold water and pat it dry with a paper towel.

3. There is no need for any spice or marinade before you put the meat onto the fire.

4. Braai the steaks on very hot coals for 6–8 minutes in total. Turn the meat between one and three times in total, and make sure both sides have faced downwards roughly the same length of time. Use a watch to time this.

5. Remove the steaks from the grid and place them on the cutting board.

6. Let them rest for a few minutes and then slice into strips. Try to slice at a 45-degree angle as this allows you to cut across the grain of the meat an additional time.

7. Pile the strips on a serving platter or in a mixing bowl and grind salt and pepper over the meat to taste.

8. Drop teaspoon-sized pieces of butter all over the meat. The butter will melt into the meat and add to the taste.

9. Serve immediately to everyone standing around the fire.

AND . . .

- If you are the fancy type that doesn't buy commercial garlic butter then prepare your own by mixing soft butter, crushed garlic, your favourite herbs, salt and pepper.
- This recipe works equally well with fillet, sirloin and rib-eye steak. If you're not making starters but a main meal then allow 250 g of meat per person.

PRIME RIB AND RIB-EYE STEAK

Two of my favourite cuts for braaing are prime rib and its refined brother, the rib-eye steak. They have lots of flavour and good marbling (fat inside the meat). This marbling will melt into the meat during the braai, adding even more flavour. Prime rib is on the bone with rib-eye essentially the same cut but off the bone. If you have the choice, go for on the bone which lends itself to dry-ageing and will in my opinion always have a superior taste to wet-aged meat. The bone will also impart flavour to the meat as it heats up during the braai.

As with all steak it should be done medium rare. If you buy the best quality meat, there is no need to mask the flavour of the meat with marinade, so keep it simple. Here are two options – you choose:

1. Bert Dessyn is the current butcher at the famous Birdstreet Butchery in Stellenbosch and years ago his father, who was the butcher at the time, told my father that mustard powder is the only way to go, on a proper steak. Since then this is how we usually do it in our family too.
2. Back in the days when National Braai Day was more an idea and less of a reality, a good friend Gys Muller used to sit around the fire with me many nights playing sounding board to my thoughts. Gys reckons the only spice a good steak needs is some fine white pepper.

WHAT YOU NEED (per person)
400-500 g steak
(250–300 g if it's off the bone)
English mustard powder and/or fine white pepper
salt

WHAT TO DO

1. Make a very hot fire. Bigger is in fact better.

2. Take the steak out the fridge and bring it to room temperature 20 minutes before the braai. If there's a lot of blood or juice in the packaging when you remove the steak, wash the meat under cold water and pat it dry with a paper towel.

3. Dust the steaks on both sides with mustard powder and/or white pepper and don't be stingy with it. Make sure the spice sticks to the meat, patting it in with your clean fingers if you have to. Let the steaks stand until your fire is burnt out and the coals are ready. Remember the dogs (when you're at home) and hyenas (when you're in the bush) and keep the meat out of their way.

4. Braai the steaks on very hot coals for about 6–8 minutes in total, turning either once or three times. Make sure both sides face downwards roughly the same length of time. Use a watch to time it. If your steaks take longer than this to become medium rare, your coals probably weren't hot enough. With prime rib, you could also balance the steaks with their bone side facing the coals for a minute.

5. Remove the steaks from the grid and put them onto pre-heated plates for each person. Eat as is or with garlic butter, mustard, or olive oil mixed with some crushed garlic and rosemary. Add salt to taste.

AND . . .

Prime rib is a serious steak for a meat connoisseur and good butcheries and steakhouses frequently dry-age it on the bone. If you can't get hold of some at your local butchery or supermarket, try to build a relationship with one of the good steakhouses in your area and buy your prime-rib steaks there. Many steakhouses in South Africa have started selling properly aged meat to the public and with a little effort you should be able to find yourself a dealer.

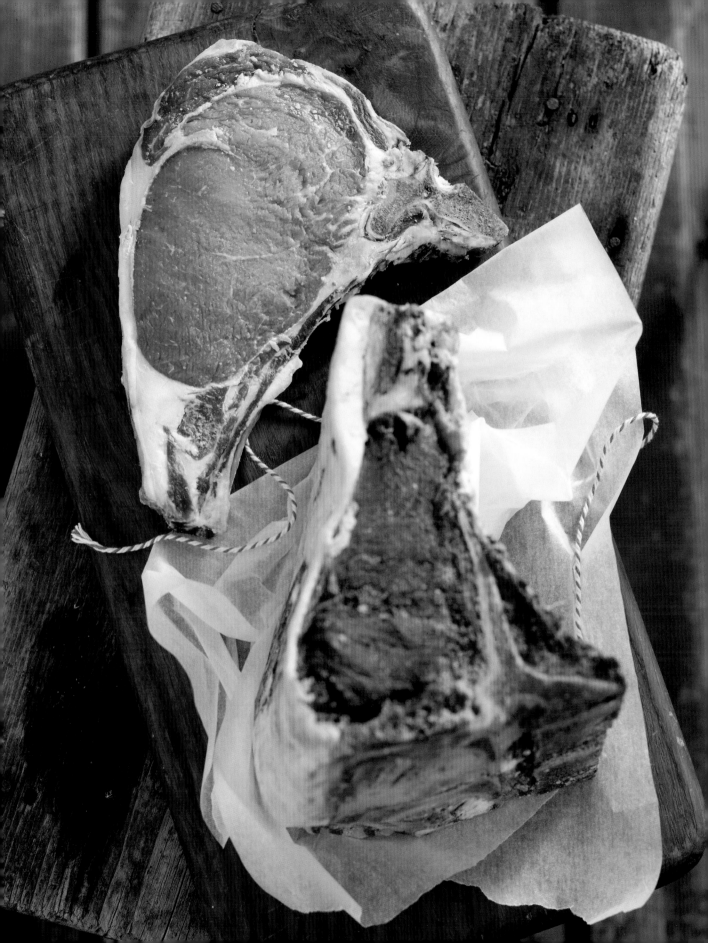

HOW TO BRAAI FILLET STEAK

A fillet is the most tender of all steaks due to the muscle's location on the beef carcass. It is situated on the belly side of the spine, and thus does very little exercise during the animal's life. It is a lean, boneless cut and contains almost no fat. On the negative side it is not the most flavoursome steak and has a tendency to dry out quickly.

Overcooking is your greatest risk when braaing a fillet. Some people like to braai fillets whole and only slice them afterwards but I prefer to cut the fillet beforehand and braai single portions. This exposes a greater surface area of the meat to the searing heat of the fire, which adds more flavour, something fillet steak needs. The steaks should be cut fairly thick in order to have a nice and juicy medium rare inside while being completely seared and sealed on the outside. To achieve this, fillet steaks naturally need to be braaied on extremely high heat.

WHAT YOU NEED (feeds 4)

1 kg piece of fillet steak
salt, pepper and mustard powder
all the ingredients for the sauce of your choice:
- mushroom (page 132)
- mustard (page 132)
- green peppercorn (page130)
- teriyaki (page 136)
- monkeygland (page 130)

WHAT TO DO

1. Cut the fillet into 5 cm thick slices. This should give you about four slices per kilogram of fillet.

2. Grind salt and pepper onto all sides of each steak then dust mustard powder onto all sides of each steak as well. Wash your hands well then use your fingers to pat the condiments onto the steaks.

3. Braai over extremely hot coals for 8–10 minutes, making sure that all sides of each steak face the coals for at least 1 minute at a time. A 5 cm-thick fillet steak will have at least four but possibly six sides.

4. Remove from the fire and let the steaks rest for a few minutes until serving. The time it takes for everybody to sit at the table, dish up their sides and pour the wine is probably enough.

5. Serve with your choice of sauce.

AND . . .

■ If you prefer to braai the fillet whole and only slice it afterwards, that is also an option. Sear it on very high heat for about 2 minutes per side (a whole fillet usually has three sides) and then adjust the heat down by either lifting the grid higher or scraping away some of the coals. Now let it braai over more gentle heat until the internal temperature of the meat reaches 57°C (and how will you know this? – by using your meat thermometer, obviously). Let it rest a few minutes and then carve. If the meat is too raw for some guests you can quickly sear the sides of their individual slices.

■ If you want your fillet steak portions to be as nicely shaped as in the photo then tie a piece of butcher string around each before braaing them.

HAMBURGERS ON THE BRAAI

The crux of the burger is the patty and the quality of that is directly dependent on the quality of the meat. Ask your butcher to give you beef mince suitable for hamburger patties that you will braai medium rare. You need 170 g per person. If the butchery does not have the right mince for your needs, ask them to grind you some mince from silverside, thick flank or whatever else they suggest. Your next best option is to buy your mince from a super-market. They often sell mince in 500 g packages, which is perfect for three patties. This may or may not be a coincidence. If you are buying supermarket mince then go for extra lean mince and braai the patties medium.

WHAT YOU NEED (per burger)

170 g good quality mince

1 hamburger roll

2 slices tomato

1 lettuce leaf

some onion rings

salt and pepper

butter

some cheddar cheese
(sliced or grated)

optional sauces

WHAT TO DO

1. Make the patties: The great thing about pure beef mince patties is that they taste exactly like pure beef mince patties. If you bought good quality mince from a proper butchery, don't add lots of condiments now. But if this makes you very nervous then you can add salt and pepper. Now go and wash your hands. Mince is much easier to handle when your hands have cold water on them. Divide the mince into same-sized balls of 170 g each and then sculpt them into patties. If you bought supermarket mince, by all means spice it.

2. Braai the patties: The biggest challenge is keeping the patties in one piece by ensuring that they don't stick to the grid. Put the patties down very gently, do not press on them, do not handle them any more than is neces-sary, and when you turn them do it with extreme care. Start on very high heat to seal them quickly, hopefully before they have the chance to 'sink' into the grid. Braai the patty for about 10 minutes in total. Once on each side during that time is enough, and twice on each side is the maximum. Don't fiddle with the patties to check whether they are sticking. As the meat starts to cook it releases fat and juices and usually loosens itself from the grid. If you always have a big problem with patties sticking to the grid then brush them with oil on both sides before the braai. If you have the time, and enough space on your braai grid, toast the insides of the rolls after you've buttered them during the final stages of your braai.

3. Assemble the burger: In its basic form you should have a buttered roll, the patty, salt and pepper, a slice or two of tomato, a lettuce leaf and a few onion rings. I consider a decent helping of (preferably aged) cheddar cheese to form part of a basic ham-burger as well.

4. Optional sauces include mustard, mayonnaise, chutney, tomato sauce and chilli sauce. For a gourmet burger, check out the sauces on pages 130 and 132 and top the patty with the mushroom, mustard, green peppercorn or monkeygland sauce.

AND . . .

In 2007, the first year that National Braai Day got mass media exposure, the wine and braai disciple Emile Joubert helped me with the PR. He skips the salad and eats his braaied hamburgers topped with cheddar cheese and a mix of mayonnaise and mustard.

ITALIAN-STYLE GIANT T-BONE (PORTERHOUSE STEAK)

As T-bone steaks have a lot of natural flavour you need to keep the condiments to a bare minimum. The most famous T-bone steak recipe in this style comes from the Tuscany region of Italy and is called 'Bistecca Fiorentina' or Florentine T-bone steak. The steaks need to be dry-aged, 3 cm thick and weigh about 800 g. The coals they are braaied on have to be from a wood fire and the steaks go onto the fire as is, with absolutely no condiments. You braai them over very high heat and while they are on the fire you are allowed to touch them only that single time when they are turned. You are not allowed to salt at all until after the turn. The only other condiment is very high quality olive oil that you drizzle over the meat after the braai.

'I like T-Bone steaks, because they are in the shape of Africa'
– Desmond Tutu

WHAT YOU NEED (feeds 2)
800 g T-bone steak, 3 cm thick
(dry-aged)
sea salt flakes
(or coarse sea salt in a grinder)
extra virgin olive oil
(very good quality, i.e. South African)

WHAT TO DO

1. Braai the steak over very hot coals for 5 minutes without touching or fiddling with it at all.

2. Use tongs or a spatula to turn it but do not use a fork or any other implement that will poke a hole in the meat.

3. Braai the T-bone for another 5 minutes on the other side and during this time sprinkle salt over the braaied side that is now facing upwards.

4. Remove the steak from the fire and put it onto a plate drizzled with olive oil (put the best-looking side facing up). Now drizzle some olive oil over the top of the meat and let it rest for 3 minutes.

5. Carve the steak: Firstly debone the sirloin and fillet and then slice them up. You can do this on a cutting board or use the plate the steak is on.

6. Serve up the slices on two plates and spoon any remaining olive oil from the plate or cutting board over the meat.

7. Make sure there is extra salt on the table that each person can add to taste.

AND . . .

■ Add variety by mixing a clove of crushed garlic and a small bit of chopped rosemary or sage into a tot of olive oil and then drizzle that over the steak after braaing.

■ This recipe lives and dies by the quality of its ingredients. Use good meat and high quality South African olive oil. I keep two bottles of olive oil in my kitchen: a more expensive and better-tasting South African one to use with recipes where the oil is used 'raw' as is, and a cheaper, big bottle of imported oil for use with recipes where the oil will be 'cooked'.

■ Get into the habit of using quality salt. Compared to the cost of meat it's really not expensive and it does make a difference to the taste of the food. Buy sea salt flakes that you sprinkle over the food or coarse sea salt that you grind over it. That fine salt in the little shaker is for fast food restaurants, not for your carefully braaied meat.

BEEF ESPETADAS FROM MADEIRA

The classic recipe, from the Portuguese island of Madeira.

WHAT YOU NEED (feeds 4)

1 kg fillet, rump or sirloin
(cut into big 5 cm cubes)

10 fresh bay leaves

4 garlic cloves

3 tots olive oil

3 tots dry sherry or port

1 tsp coarse sea salt

1 tsp black pepper

4 skewers

WHAT TO DO

1. Crush the garlic and roughly shred the bay leaves with your clean hands.

2. Combine the crushed garlic and shredded bay leaves with the oil, sherry/port, salt and pepper.

3. Pour this marinade over the meat cubes in a marinating bowl and using your hands toss thoroughly to coat all sides of the meat. The meat doesn't need to swim in marinade, it should just be coated.

4. Cover and let the meat marinate for at least 5 hours, but preferably overnight.

5. Skewer the meat and include pieces of the bay leaves here and there on each skewer.

6. Braai over very hot coals for about 8–10 minutes until medium rare, turning about three times. If there is left-over marinade you can baste the meat with it during this time (but not right at the end, as that will mean you have raw meat marinade on your meat). The easiest way to braai espetadas is to place them in a hinged grid.

7. With this recipe you do not have to let the meat rest before serving. Serve with fresh bread (Portuguese rolls or *roosterkoek*) and mop up the sauce from your plate with the fresh bread.

AND...

■ The original recipe from Madeira uses Madeira wine but a dry sherry or dry port is close enough.

■ Bay leaves, on the other hand, are the crux of this recipe and you can't replace them with any other leaves or herbs. Originally the meat was actually skewered onto freshly cut bay branches as I did in the photo, but I don't expect you to do that. Fresh bay leaves are better than dried ones, so plant a bay tree in your garden.

SIRLOIN PEPPER STEAK FLAMBÉ

Right in the middle of the Moordenaars Karoo, somewhere between Laingsburg and Sutherland, is a farm called De Fonteine. In the mountains of that farm is a kloof with a braai spot and when we braai steaks there, we do it without a grid. We search the veld for a big, flat rock and position it in the flames of the fire. With flames licking around the sides, the steak is seared straight on the rock. When I'm at home in the city with no big flat rocks lying around, I just use my fireproof steel pan which is great, as it saves all the juices and sauce which can then be served with the steak. Check out the photo of the *Bratkartoffeln* on page 161 to see what the pan looks like.

WHAT YOU NEED (feeds 4)

4 matured sirloin steaks
(200–300 g per person for mains)

2 tots olive oil (or butter)

1 tot brandy

salt and black pepper

about 3 tots cream

fireproof steel or cast-iron pan

tongs, a spatula or a wooden spoon

WHAT TO DO

1. Grind salt and pepper onto both sides of each steak and use your fingers to pat it in. Don't be shy with the pepper.

2. Place the pan over the flames and make sure it stands evenly and securely. Speciality catering shops sell steel pans that can be used on fires.

3. Add olive oil to the pan. If you don't want to burn your eyebrows you might want to do this before putting the pan on the flames.

4. As soon as the oil is really hot, place the steaks in the pan, which is on the fire. Take care not to get splashed with the oil. I usually use braai tongs to get some distance between myself and that boiling hot oil in the pan.

5. Turn the meat after about 3 minutes then remove the pan from the fire after another 3 minutes (for very thin steak in a shorter time, for very thick steak longer). Leave the steak in the pan. Add the brandy to the pan, take the pan back to the flames and tilt it slightly so that the brandy can catch fire.

6. As soon as the fire in the pan has died down, remove the steaks from the pan and put them on the serving plates, where they can rest for a few minutes.

7. Pour the cream into the pan and use tongs, a spatula or a wooden spoon to scrape off any bits sticking to the bottom of the pan and mix that with the cream. As soon as the cream boils and starts to thicken, pour this sauce (essentially consisting of olive oil, meat juice, salt, pepper and cream) from the pan over each of the steaks. This step is obviously not possible when you braai the steaks on a rock.

8. Season with extra salt if needed.

AND . . .

■ As this meal is prepared entirely on flames, it also works well as a starter while you wait for the fire to burn out and form coals. In that case, slice the meat up after it has rested a few minutes and then toss back into the pan with the sauce. You can serve up straight from the pan.

■ This recipe works equally well with rump, fillet slices and rib-eye steaks.

■ Sirloin steak is also known as entrecôte.

STEAK PREGO ROLL

Considering how awesome it tastes this is a very straightforward recipe and I suggest you simply learn it off by heart. It will save you a lot of time and effort as in future you won't need to find a Portuguese restaurant every time you crave a steak prego roll.

WHAT YOU NEED (makes 4 rolls)

4 steaks like rump or sirloin, 150-200 g each (as they need to fit onto rolls, buying bigger steaks and slicing them into pieces also works)

4 Portuguese rolls

butter

2 tomatoes

4 lettuce leaves

peri-peri sauce (page 134)

WHAT TO DO

1. Make the peri-peri sauce.

2. Gently pound each steak with a meat mallet to make it tender and better able to absorb the marinade. As you will eat the steak straight from the roll, you want it nice and soft so the average set of teeth can bite clean through it.

3. Place the steaks in a marinating bowl and pour some of the peri-peri sauce over them. Flip them over using a tool like a spoon and get some sauce on the other sides of the steaks as well. You want to coat both sides of each steak but it is not necessary for the steaks to swim in the sauce.

4. Cover the bowl and place in a cool place like a fridge. Go and light the fire.

5. Slice the rolls, butter them and place two slices of tomato and one lettuce leaf in each.

6. When the coals are ready, and they must be hot to very hot, braai the steaks until medium rare. For a thin 150 g steak this could take about 5 minutes.

7. Remove the steaks from the grid and place one in each of the prepared rolls.

8. Let your guests add extra peri-peri sauce until their prego is as hot as they like it.

AND . . .

For this meal those vacuum-packed portions of supermarket rump and sirloin steaks are perfect. They usually come in portions over 300 g so buy one or more of those and slice them into the desired number of pieces.

OXTAIL *POTJIE*

Collagen is a connective tissue, which helps to hold the muscle fibres in meat together. When cooked in a *potjie*, collagen dissolves into gelatine, which leads to the rich, deep flavour of a typical *potjie* dish. Less tender cuts of meats have greater amounts of collagen than tender ones and are thus better suited to making *potjie*. A cut of meat that is too tender will fall apart during the long cooking time and will also not develop the rich taste of a meat like oxtail.

When cooking something like an oxtail *potjie* go for a slow and gentle simmer allowing the meat fibres to separate without them contracting and toughening up as will happen when you boil the meat rapidly.

WHAT YOU NEED (feeds 6)

1.5 kg oxtail pieces
1 tot olive oil
1 tot flour
2 onions (chopped)
6 carrots (peeled and chopped)
15 cm celery sticks (finely chopped)
1 potato (finely chopped)
2 bay leaves
2 garlic cloves (chopped)
½ tot salt
1 tsp black pepper
5 cloves
4 tomatoes (chopped)

1 cup water
1 cup red wine or port
1 cup beef stock
if you have thyme in your herb garden, a bit of that

WHAT TO DO

1. Fry the oxtail pieces in the olive oil for a few minutes until they are browned. If they cannot fit onto the bottom of the pot all at the same time then do this in batches. For this part, the pot can be on hot coals or even flames.

2. Remove the oxtail pieces from the pot, dust with the flour and store somewhere safe.

3. Now fry the onion, carrot, celery and potato in the liquid that is left at the bottom of the pot.

4. As soon as the onions start to go golden, add all the remaining ingredients, including the oxtail pieces, to the pot. Stir all the ingredients around and put on the lid. Move the pot further away from the fire and place a few coals under it, or scrape away some coals or logs from the pot.

5. Simmer gently for 4–5 hours with the lid on. The food is ready if the meat comes off the bone when you test it with a fork and the sauce starts to thicken. If the pot runs dry during this time, add more liquid in the form of water, wine or beef stock (you'll obviously have to remove the lid now and again to make these observations). If after 3 or 4 hours you feel that there is still too much liquid in the pot, remove the lid and let the *potjie*

simmer without the lid until the liquid has reduced or thickened enough for your liking.

6. Serve with parsley-flavoured mashed potatoes. Alternatively add peeled and halved potatoes or baby potatoes to the pot for the last 90 minutes of cooking time.

WHAT TO DO FOR PARSLEY-FLAVOURED MASHED POTATO

1. Wash 6 medium-to-large potatoes, then boil them in salted water until very soft. When their skins start to burst you will know they are ready.

2. You don't need to peel the potatoes; the skin adds to the taste. Discard all the water from the pot and use a masher to mash the potatoes.

3. Stir in two tots of butter or cream and two tots of chopped, fresh parsley. Add salt and pepper to taste.

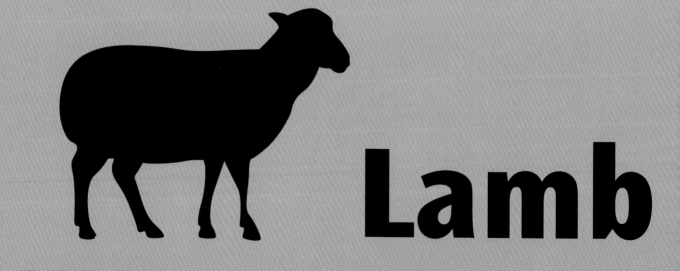

Lamb

I n South Africa there are two types of sheep: those bred for meat – the most famous one is the Dorper, and those bred for meat and wool – of which the Merino is the best-known. Roughly a third of the lamb meat we eat comes from the former type and the rest from the latter. The type a specific farmer breeds depends on a number of factors, with geographical location the most important. 'A' grade meat from both types tastes great and is similar enough that we're not going to discuss the differences.

Even though equal numbers of male and female lambs are born on a sheep farm, about two-thirds of all lamb meat that we eat comes from male lambs. This is because significantly more females than males are kept for reproductive purposes. Again, differences in taste and texture are negligible for the purposes of this book. In summary, whether the lamb that you eat is from a Dorper or a Merino and whether it's from a male or female makes very little difference.

But this is the important part:

Lamb meat comes from young animals. In the sheep grading system they are 'A' grade, and to achieve that grading they should not have real teeth yet. As soon as they get two real teeth they are classified 'AB' and are no longer lambs. The meat from these older animals is known as mutton. After 'AB' the next rating is 'B' and then 'C'. These are all mutton. According to the definition then, all lamb is 'A' grade as anything else is classified as mutton.

Lambs are usually slaughtered somewhere between 3 and 7 months of age, and the average carcass you see at the butcher weighs between 16 and 24 kilograms. In general, the younger it is slaughtered, the less it weighs.

Those purple stamps that mark the grade on the carcass don't use just one A on a lamb but rather a long vertical line of three As. Some people mistakenly call this 'triple A' lamb but there is no such thing. This line of AAA marking simply means it is an A grade animal – in other words it is a lamb. The only other rating refers to the covering of fat on the carcass. A0 means that the meat contains no fat and A1 means that it has very little fat. Both will be quite dry on the braai. A6 on the other hand means that the meat contains a lot of fat, some of which you will probably need to discard after paying meat prices for it. When you buy lamb chops for the braai then, go for A2 or A3, as that is the best both in taste and value.

LAMB LOIN CHOPS

A lamb loin chop is one of the true highlights of braaing. It is exactly like a T-bone steak, only cut from a lamb. It's also the most expensive cut of lamb. Keep the recipe and braaing simple so that you don't overpower its natural taste. Make sure you remove the meat from the fire in time, before it dries out.

WHAT YOU NEED (feeds 4)

12 lamb loin chops

2 cloves garlic

1 tot fresh rosemary (or thyme or oregano, see options discussion at end of recipe)

1 tot lemon juice (freshly squeezed)

2 tots olive oil

coarse sea salt and black pepper

WHAT TO DO

1. Make one or two small cuts through the fat strip of each chop. This will keep the chops from bending as the fat strip cooks and contracts. It will also show your guests that you paid attention to detail during the preparation of their meal.

2. Chop or crush the garlic, pull the rosemary leaves off the stalk and squeeze the lemon juice. Combine this with the olive oil and toss the chops in it ensuring all sides of all the chops are coated with marinade.

3. Let the meat marinate for as long as it takes your fire to burn out and form coals. If you want to marinate the meat overnight do so but then only add the lemon juice once you light the fire.

4. Braai the chops over hot coals for 8–12 minutes until they reach that point between medium rare and medium where lamb tastes best. Lamb loin chops vary widely in size and the heat of your fire will also play a role in how long they take to braai. Remember the golden rule: if you think it's ready, it probably is. Some exceptionally small lamb chops are ready after 6 minutes, so just use your common sense.

5. Grind the salt and pepper onto the chops while they are braaing. If you are lazy you can also do it before they go onto the braai, but doing it during the braai will cause someone to ask you what spices you are adding. You can then impress everybody listening in by saying that you're only adding salt and pepper, as you like to keep it simple with lamb loin chops.

AND . . .

■ The one additional spice that is always good on lamb is crushed coriander. Buy some dried coriander seeds, crush them using your pestle and mortar and sprinkle on the chops before or during the braai.

■ Thicker lamb loin chops should be braaied with three sides of the meat facing the coals. These are the two 'normal' sides as well at the strip of fat on the edge. Braai the two normal sides first and then line the chops up, balancing them to lean against each other so that their strips of fat face the coals and become crisp.

■ You can also put the chops side by side and put a skewer through them. Braai the fat edge first for a minute or three. Then remove the skewer and braai the flat sides of the chops.

■ I first started making this recipe using thyme but in South African braai culture it's also quite popular to use rosemary in combination with olive oil and garlic on lamb. Then I learnt something else at the Greek wedding of Dan Nicholl and Dimitra Kouvelakis when a relative of the bride explained to me that I've got it all wrong and the only way to do this recipe is to use oregano. I suggest you try out all three options and decide which one you prefer. Just remember to go easy on the herbs and retain the natural flavour of the lamb.

BRAAIED LAMB RIB

For many passionate fans, this is as good as braaing gets. It's also one of the cuts of meat that is absolutely, without a doubt, best prepared on the braai. Braaing lamb rib is exactly the opposite of braaing steak. With lamb rib you need gentle heat and it's a slow process. Due to the layers of fat that are naturally present inside the rib, there is little danger of it drying out. Your risk is going too fast and burning the outside before it's ready.

Ask your butcher to prepare the required number of lamb ribs for you to braai. He will need to trim away the loose flap, fat and sinews. He might also cut strategically through some of the bones to make it easier to eat and will possibly cut a crosshatch pattern into the fat or skin side of the rib so that you get nice little blocks of crackling on that side of the rib once it has been braaied.

WHAT YOU NEED
(feeds 2)
1 lamb rib
½ lemon
1 tot Worcestershireshire sauce
coarse sea salt
freshly ground black pepper
brush made from rosemary twigs
(or a kitchen brush)

WHAT TO DO

1. Twenty minutes before you want to start braaing, squeeze some of the lemon juice onto both sides of the rib. Take care to remove any pips that fall onto the meat. Also grind sea salt onto it. If the salt does not stick, use one of your recently washed hands to pat it onto the meat.

2. Place the ribs on the braai grid and start to braai. You should braai these ribs for an absolute minimum of 1 hour, preferably 1½ hours. To accomplish this you obviously need gentle heat, which means a very high grid and mild coals. Another popular option is to use a hinged grid and place it vertically next to the fire or coals where just enough heat will reach it to melt the fat and crisp the meat in your allocated 90 minutes. You can braai a rib in less time but it will be less tender.

3. When you judge the meat to be almost (80%) ready, use a brush made from rosemary twigs to paint the Worcestershireshire sauce onto both sides of the meat. If you're too lazy to make this brush, use your normal food brush.

4. To check whether the ribs are done, grab the edge of one of the bones and tear the rib away from the rest. It should be relatively easy to pull it off.

5. Remove the ribs from the fire and place on a cutting board or in a bowl. Cut them with either a knife or kitchen scissors. Serve with salt and pepper and eat them with your hands.

AND . . .

■ Instead of using Worcestershireshire sauce, try sprinkling 1 tot of crushed coriander seeds on both sides of the ribs.
■ If you don't feel like braaing the rib for 90 minutes, bake it in your oven at 140°C for 90 minutes in a covered dish. Then braai it over the coals for 20 minutes in the way you would braai chicken. Baste with the lemon juice and Worcestershire sauce during this time, adding salt as required.
■ Never pre-boil ribs in a pot of water as they will lose a lot of their natural juices and flavour to the water.

LAMB CURRY SOSATIES

The sosaties in this recipe taste great and the recipe is basically foolproof. Curry sosaties is a typical South African dish, so be sure to include it on the menu when you have foreign guests who you want to impress.

WHAT YOU NEED (feeds 10)

2 kg lamb (deboned and cubed – at a stretch the marinade will be enough for 2.5 kg meat)

2 tots oil or butter

2 onions (chopped)

3 cloves garlic (crushed)

peeled and grated ginger (equal to the garlic in volume)

2 tots curry powder

½ tot turmeric

2 cups brown vinegar

450 g tin fine or smooth apricot jam

½ tot salt

4–8 fresh bay leaves (torn)

dried apricots and pieces of onion and peppers (optional)

10 skewers

closed, hinged grid

WHAT TO DO

1. Fry the onions in the oil for about 4 minutes until they are soft and golden but not brown.

2. Add the garlic, ginger, curry powder and turmeric, and fry for another 2 minutes.

3. Stir in the vinegar, jam and salt and heat until boiling.

4. Remove from the heat and let the marinade cool down to room temperature. This takes a few hours.

5. Prepare the meat: Debone the lamb and remove all silver skin and sinews. Then cut the meat into cubes of about 3 × 3 cm, but remember this is not an exact science. You can also ask your butcher to prepare 2 kg of meat in this manner.

6. Place the cubed meat into a marinating bowl, add the torn bay leaves and pour the cooled-down marinade over the meat. Toss thoroughly and make sure you coat all the meat. Cover the bowl.

7. Marinate for at least 12 hours, but 2 or 3 days is better. Stir the meat every 8–12 hours during this time.

8. Skewer the meat while the fire is burning. If you like, you can also add dried apricots and pieces of onion and peppers between the meat cubes when you are skewering.

9. Braai for about 10 minutes over hot coals, turning a few times. The easiest way to do this is to clamp all the sosaties in a closed, hinged grid.

AND . . .

- The sauce takes a few hours to cool down to room temperature. If you have an office job, it is a good idea to make the sauce in the evening, let it stand overnight, and then pour the marinade over the meat the next morning.
- The classic curry sosatie is made with lamb but there are other options. A combination of lamb, beef and pork is also good. Try to alternate between the different types of meat when you skewer them, but don't be too fussy about it. The recipe also works well with venison and I've made some very tasty sosaties using this marinade with a half-and-half mix of lamb and springbok.

BRAAIED TANDOORI LAMB CHOPS

A tandoor is a clay oven tradi-
tionally used in Eastern cooking,
and tandoori refers to any food
cooked in a tandoor oven. A fire
of wood or coal is made inside the
oven and the food is exposed to
direct heat. The smoke from the
fire, and the smoke from the food
juices and fat dripping onto the
coals, all add to the flavour. Very
similar, you could say, to a braai!
And as we all know, anything
tastes better when it is braaied!

Masala is a blend of spices
usually found in Indian cooking.
A typical masala would include
spices such as paprika, cloves,
chilli, coriander, garlic, onion,
cumin, cardamom, nutmeg, mustard, turmeric and star anise, all in
dried, powdered form.

WHAT YOU NEED (feeds 6)

16–20 lamb chops (lamb rib chops
work well for this recipe)

500 ml plain yoghurt

**2 tots tandoori masala or tikka
masala** (or whatever 'special' masala
your local spice merchant suggests
when you tell him you want to make
tandoori lamb chops; otherwise, just buy
normal masala at a supermarket)

1 tot lemon juice

1 tot chopped garlic and ginger (you
can buy a pre-mix of this from some
supermarkets – I wouldn't use it but
braaing should be fun, so if you're in a
rush or feeling lazy, go for it)

salt

WHAT TO DO

1. Trim excess fat off the chops but
leave some on for flavour.

2. Make the marinade by mixing
the yoghurt, masala, lemon juice and
garlic and ginger together in a bowl.
Use your recently washed hands or a
spoon to toss the chops around in the
marinade, ensuring all the chops are
coated.

3. Leave them to marinate for a few
hours or a day.

4. Braai over hot coals (but not too
hot) for about 10–12 minutes until
that point between medium rare and
medium where lamb chops taste their
best. Grind salt onto both sides of the
chops while they are braaing.

AND . . .

You can also make tandoori lamb
sosaties. Use cubes of lamb from the
leg or shoulder, marinate as above and
skewer them just before braaing.

RACK OF LAMB

The bone and the nice layer of fat make this cut ideally suited to a slow and gentle braai and those same two reasons make this a very tasty cut of meat. While you can braai a lamb loin chop and most steaks in less than 10 minutes, this dish gives you the opportunity to actually spend time around the fire while you are braaing. Once it is braaied and while it is resting before you carve it, a rack of lamb also makes an impressive centrepiece on your table.

WHAT YOU NEED (feeds 3-4)

rack of lamb (8 to 9 rib chops per rack)
olive oil
oregano, rosemary or thyme
coarse sea salt
freshly ground black pepper
meat thermometer

WHAT TO DO

1. Ask your butcher to prepare the rack of lamb for braaing. Importantly, he should use his meat saw to make a small cut through the backbone between each rib bone so that you can easily carve the rack into individual chops. In addition, he could do the following:

- French the rack, which means to clean the tips of each bone. Ask him to French it just slightly, so that he doesn't cut away half the meat. As shown in the photograph, you want the tip of each bone to be clean so that you are left with an attractive rack with meat that comes off the bone easily.
- Remove the membrane on the bone side of the rack.
- Cut a crosshatch pattern into the layer of fat on the outside which makes it easier to braai and makes you look like the type of expert who uses this book.

2. Once back at home, pour a thin layer of olive oil on the meat and sprinkle with the salt, pepper and herb(s) of your choice. Use your recently washed hands to rub these condiments into the meat. It's up to you whether or not you rest the meat after this before you braai it. The meat should be at room temperature when you start the braai, so take it out of the fridge when you light the fire.

3. A rack of lamb is a pretty impressive, enjoyable piece of meat to braai. It's somewhere between braaing a lamb chop and a lamb rib, and you should do it over hot coals. Take your time. A small rack can be ready in

20 minutes but a big one can take up to 40 minutes. This range in braai time comes down to wide variations in size and is also a question of how aggressively your rack was Frenched and whether it was at room temperature or straight from the fridge when you started braaing it. For most of the braai time, the rack will face fat-layer side or rib-bone side down, but also braai the rack standing on the flat-bone side at times.

4. The meat is ready when the internal temperature reads 63°C in the middle of the thickest part. If you don't own a meat thermometer, rather remove the meat too early than too late. If any or all of the chops need more braaing when you cut them, you can always return them to the fire as individual chops.

5. Let the meat rest for at least 5 minutes before cutting.

AND . . .

If the exposed bones at the tip of each rib bone start to burn, wrap them individually in foil.

CURRY LAMB CHOPS

The ingredients of this marinade and the long marinating time mean you can use slightly tougher lamb chops like leg, chump and thick rib to make this recipe. After 2 to 3 days in the marinade the meat will be amazingly tender and full of flavour. The attentive reader will notice that the ingredients of this recipe are very similar to those of the curry sosaties and the reason for that is simple: the marinade and the result are awesome!

WHAT YOU NEED (feeds 6–8)

2–2.5 kg lamb chops (I prefer leg but chump or thick rib also work well)

2 tots oil or butter

2 onions (chopped)

3 cloves garlic (crushed)

peeled and grated ginger (equal to the garlic in volume)

2 tots curry powder

½ tot turmeric

½ tot salt

2 cups brown vinegar

450 g tin fine or smooth apricot jam

4 bay leaves (torn)

WHAT TO DO

1. Fry the onions in the oil for about 4 minutes until they are soft and golden but not brown.

2. Add the garlic, ginger, curry powder and turmeric and fry for another 2 minutes.

3. Stir in the vinegar, jam and salt and heat until boiling.

4. Remove from the heat and let the marinade cool down to room temperature. This takes a few hours.

5. Place the chops in a marinating bowl, add the torn bay leaves and pour the cooled-down marinade over the meat. Stir thoroughly ensuring all sides of the chops are in contact with marinade. Cover the bowl.

6. Marinate for at least 24 hours, but 2 or 3 days is better. Turn the chops every 8–12 hours during this time.

7. Braai for about 8–10 minutes on hot coals and serve with brandy and coke.

AND . . .

The braaiers in De Aar use a similar recipe to this one for their curry lamb chops and agree that giving the meat 3 days in the marinade is the way to go – so if you have the time, don't settle for 24 hours.

GREEK LEG OF LAMB BRAAIED THE SOUTH AFRICAN WAY

The ingredients are pure and basic, designed to bring out the natural lamb flavour. A relatively long braai time allows the meat to develop a great taste. When braaing a leg of lamb over direct heat it should be deboned – and the easiest way to debone a leg of lamb is to ask your butcher to do it.

WHAT YOU NEED
(feeds about 6)

1 deboned leg of lamb
5 cloves garlic
1 tot thyme (you can also add some oregano and rosemary if you feel like it)
½ cup olive oil
1 lemon
½ tot ground black pepper
salt
meat thermometer

WHAT TO DO

1. Make sure the meat is more or less the same thickness by laying it out on a chopping board and gently flattening the thicker parts with a meat mallet or any other suitable object (like a cheap bottle of wine).

2. Prepare the marinade: Finely chop the garlic and herbs. Mix this with the olive oil, juice from the lemon and black pepper.

3. Marinate the meat in a covered bowl or plastic bag, in the fridge, for 24–48 hours. I find that it also works well to pour the marinade over the meat and then to roll the meat up and wrap it tightly in cling wrap. In a rush a shorter marinating time is fine, but an overnight session gives the flavours time to develop.

4. Braai over medium-to-hot coals for roughly 30 minutes, with a bigger piece possibly taking 40 minutes. Paint the meat with any leftover marinade and also grind salt over the meat during this time. The idea is to completely seal the outsides and have the inside medium rare to medium. Remove from fire when the thickest part has an internal temperature of 63°C on your meat thermometer.

5. Let the meat rest for 10 minutes before carving it. During this time the juices will settle and the meat will also continue to cook to a point still slightly below medium.

AND . . .

■ Some people like to make small cuts in the meat and push the garlic and herbs into them. I believe there's enough contact between the marinade and the surface of the meat for the garlic flavour to go into the lamb. If you want a stronger garlic flavour, use more garlic in the marinade.

■ By braaing over hot coals and being careful not to burn the meat, it's quite possible to braai a butterflied leg of lamb in 30 minutes. If you're worried the meat will burn, lower the heat and make it 40 or 50 minutes. Or, get clever and use a meat thermometer, then you can braai on medium-to-hot coals until the middle of the thickest part of the meat reaches 63°C and be sure it's perfect.

LAMB SHANK (OR LAMB NECK) *POTJIE*

A lamb *potjie* can be made with whole shanks, neck chops or any other pieces marked for stewing. They will all taste roughly the same, but presentation-wise whole shanks are the way to go. Stay away from loin and rib chops for *potjie*. They are too soft and will fall apart.

WHAT YOU NEED (feeds 6)

1.5 kg lamb meat on the bone (shanks, neck chops or stewing lamb – if you're using shanks, get one shank for each person you intend to serve even though this might weigh slightly more)

olive oil or butter

2 onions (chopped or sliced)

3 cloves garlic (chopped)

ginger (chopped and equal to garlic in volume)

1 stick celery (chopped)

1 tot of your favourite masala (optional)

salt and pepper

1 kg tomatoes (chopped with or without skin)

500 g potatoes (baby potatoes – whole; big potatoes – peeled and halved or quartered)

about 5 carrots (peeled and cut in to chunks)

any other interesting vegetables on hand (could be green beans, baby marrow, mushrooms, peppers, sweet potato, etc, anything really)

fresh herbs (like parsley, sage, rosemary, thyme, oregano)

½ cup cream (optional)

WHAT TO DO

1. Place the pot on the fire and heat the olive oil or butter. Add the onions, garlic, ginger and celery and fry for 2 minutes. To give the meal that extra bit of personality, also add the masala. As with all *potjies*, you can do this frying part on flames and the rest of the time you should keep the *potjie* simmering by placing a few coals underneath it.

2. Add the lamb, and brown on all sides. If the pot is too warm and the meat is burning, add a few tots of wine or water. Grind salt and pepper onto the meat during this time and when the meat is browned, add the tomatoes.

3. Put the lid onto the pot, and gently simmer for 1 hour.

4. After an hour add the potatoes and carrots. Also add all other vegetables you are using that have to be eaten cooked (e.g. sweet potato and pumpkin). Grind salt and pepper onto the top layer of what you see.

5. Do not stir the pot but gently ensure there is enough liquid in the bottom, and that it's not burning. If unsure, add a bit more wine or water.

6. Replace the lid and simmer for another hour.

7. Now add all the vegetables that you can eat raw (e.g. mushrooms, baby marrows, peppers).

8. Replace the lid and simmer for another half an hour. The total cooking time should be 3 hours.

9. Remove the pot from the fire. Add cream and fresh herbs 5 minutes before serving with rice or, and I prefer this, fresh baguettes.

AND . . .

■ This is a basic lamb *potjie* recipe. From here you can experiment and change it as you wish.

■ Do not stir the pot at any time. This will break the vegetables and make you look like an amateur.

■ At the end of the process, just before serving, you should have minimal free-flowing liquid in the pot and a nice thick sauce at the bottom. We are not making soup.

■ 5 minutes before serving you can add half a cup of fresh cream to the pot.

■ This recipe also works well with venison. Simply add one cup of dried fruit to the pot.

LAMB BURGERS

Lamb mince is usually made from the neck, breast, thick rib, flank or trimmings from the more popular braai cuts. Unfortunately it's quite hard to get hold of and not always available at butcheries. Lamb burgers are thus an opportunistic meal. Ask the butcher whether he has lamb mince on hand and, if he does, cancel your other plans.

WHAT YOU NEED

(makes 6 burgers)

6 hamburger rolls (or pita breads)

For the patties:

1 kg lamb mince

5 ml coriander seeds

5 ml cumin seeds

5 ml salt

5 ml black pepper

2 garlic cloves

1 smallish onion (or half a big one, finely chopped)

1 tot fresh mint

1 tot fresh parsley

1 tot fresh oregano

olive oil

For the tzatziki:

1 cup Greek yoghurt (if you can't find Greek yoghurt, go for whatever plain yoghurt is available that is furthest removed from fat-free yoghurt)

½ cucumber (chopped)

1 tot olive oil

2 finely chopped garlic cloves (more if, like me, you like garlic)

1 tot chopped mix of fresh parsley and mint

salt and pepper

1 lemon

For the salad:

½ cucumber (the other half)

2 big or 12 cherry tomatoes

200 g feta cheese

WHAT TO DO

1. Make the tzatziki sauce by combining all its ingredients and then adding salt, pepper and a few squeezes of lemon juice to taste.

2. Make the salad by chopping and combining the tomatoes, cucumber and feta cheese. Add a bit of olive oil to give it that nice shine.

3. Use a pestle and mortar and crush the coriander, cumin, salt, pepper and garlic.

4. Finely chop the onion, mint, parsley and oregano. Mix this with the lamb mince and all the crushed ingredients of the previous step. Make 6 patties from the spiced meat and put them on a plate.

5. Lightly brush the patties with olive oil on each side before braaing them on hot coals. This improves the taste, helps them not to stick to the grid, and some of the oil might cause flames to flare up which helps to seal the outside of the patties.

6. Braai the patties for about 10 minutes until medium and then remove from the fire and let them rest for a few minutes.

7. Serve on a roll with salad and tzatziki sauce.

AND . . .

■ If you wet your hands in cold water before working with mincemeat there will be less chance of the meat sticking to your hands.

■ If you can't find fresh mint, parsley or oregano, then leave out what you don't have and make a note to upgrade your herb garden next weekend. These are basic herbs that grow easily in most parts of South Africa. You really should have them.

■ Original tzatziki recipes tell you to first salt the cucumber to dry it out and make the sauce firmer. You don't really have to do it but now you know, just in case you ever end up discussing tzatziki sauce with a distant relative of the Greek bride at a friend's wedding.

HOW TO SPIT A WHOLE LAMB

To state the obvious, if you want to spit a lamb you'll need two things not normally present at your everyday braai, namely a whole lamb and a spit. Of the two a spit is usually the tougher one to get hold of. A spit comes in various designs but the basic function is the same. It is a piece of equipment that you tie a lamb carcass to and use to suspend that lamb over the coals for a few hours. You must be able to turn the lamb on the spit and expose the lamb to the heat of the coals at various angles.

If you struggle to locate a spit, start by asking your local butcher. Failing that, ask the local sports clubs, schools and churches. In short, the type of organisations that typically host spit braais usually own or know where to locate a spit.

Now for the lamb: Remember, you want A grade lamb. B grade and C grade imply that it's an older animal and not really a lamb, the proverbial 'mutton dressed as lamb'. The fat covering of a lamb is rated from 0-6 with the ideal grading being an A2 or A3. On average you need 500 g of carcass weight per person, as this will give you more than 250 g of edible meat per person in the end. For example, a 15 kg lamb on the spit can feed 30 people and a 20 kg lamb on the spit can feed 40 people. In the industry a 17-18 kg lamb

is considered optimal. For most normal people it works best to fetch the lamb from the butcher on the morning of your spit braai as whole lambs don't fit into the majority of household fridges.

You will need a lot of coals and it's best to manufacture these by making a separate fire on the side. For the entire duration of the braai you need a bed of coals under the leg area of the lamb and another bed of coals under the shoulder area of the lamb but for under the rib part you only need coals for the last hour. Assuming that a bed of coals lasts 30 minutes and that your lamb will take 4 hours, you need coals from, and thus wood for, at least 18 proper fires but it's never a bad idea to have to reserve stock. Make the first big fire about 40 minutes before you want to start braaing. Continuously feed it with wood over the next few hours and use a spade to shovel coals from there to under your lamb during the braai.

WHAT YOU NEED (feeds 35)

17-18 kg whole lamb
olive oil
quite a lot of coarse sea salt
quite a lot of crushed black pepper
quite a lot of dried oregano
tinfoil
wire and wire cutter

WHAT TO DO

1. For best results, make sure your lamb is at room temperature when it goes onto the spit. Remove it from the fridge or fetch it from the butcher a few hours in advance and cover it with a big cloth (a clean, old sheet works well).

2. Wash all parts of the spit that will touch the lamb. You will be surprised how often spits are left dirty until the next spit braai.

3. Tie the lamb to the spit using wire and a wire cutter (a great opportunity to use your multi-tool!) You need to run the wire around bone at each point that you tie it, as the meat will not hold when the lamb starts to cook, and your meal will end up in the fire and more roasted than you want it to be. First secure the spine to the spit pole lengthwise in at least four places. Then secure the four legs to the two rods running crosswise. These two cross rods will usually be adjustable to the size of your lamb. Tie the lamb to the spit on its inside (belly side).

4. Paint or smear the olive oil all over the lamb and then rub it with the salt, pepper and oregano mix. You do not need to measure out the rub exactly – simply mix ½ salt, ¼ pepper and ¼ oregano.

5. Place tinfoil around the rib area of the lamb. For the first 2 hours, you want the legs and shoulders exposed to the direct heat and radiation of the coals but not the ribs, as they are much thinner and will dry out.

6. Place the lamb on the spit and rake coals to the area under the shoulders and under the legs. For the next

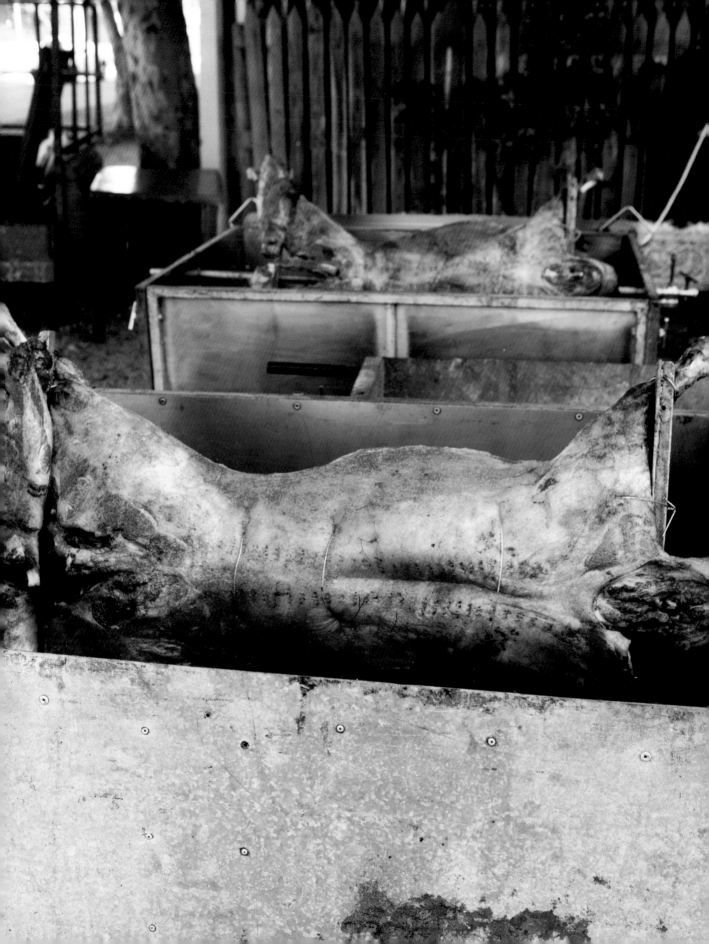

HOW TO SPIT A WHOLE LAMB (CONTINUED)

2 hours, turn the lamb on a regular basis and top up the coals whenever it seems that there is not enough cooking action.

7. After 2 to 2½ hours, remove the tinfoil covering the middle rib area of the lamb. At this stage you can also rake a few coals to that middle area.

8. If you want to destroy the natural taste of the lamb, the 2½ hour mark is also the time you can start basting it with whatever sauce you prefer. I do not advise basting the lamb, and so I haven't included a recipe for a basting sauce here. But, if you are going to baste then only start now as starting earlier just means that the basting coat will burn.

9. Instead of basting the lamb, go for a natural approach. Throw some rosemary branches onto the coals. They will start smoking and this smoke will infuse the lamb with a complementary natural flavour.

10. A lamb on the spit is ready to eat after an average of 3 to 4 hours. The exact time depends on factors such as: heat of coals; height of meat; wind (a cross wind can blow away a lot of your heat and lengthen the braaing time); whether your meat came straight from a fridge or was at room temperature when you placed it on the spit; and whether your spit is completely exposed or has one or more sides that are closed to the level of the lamb, which obviously steers more heat towards the meat (as with the spit in the photos).

11. To test whether it is done, stick a knife in the thick area where the spine, shoulder and neck join. You are going to carve up the meat anyway so this does no real harm at this stage. If the juice runs clear, the lamb is ready. Alternatively use a meat thermometer and check that the internal temperature of the thickest parts is 63°C. Another tactic to employ if you are not sure whether the lamb is ready is to simply start carving off all parts that are ready while the lamb is still on the spit. When you reach the parts closer to the bone that are still a bit raw then simply leave that meat on the carcass and continue braaing it. This ploy also works well when you have a lamb that will feed 35 people with only 20 present as it delivers a steady flow of freshly braaied meat for everyone's second round.

12. Now it's time to carve the lamb. Don't be intimidated by the size. As with all meat it's better to rest it a few minutes before carving. When you carve, try to cut across the grain. If at first you don't succeed, don't despair – you have a whole lamb to practise on. The end goal is simply to get all the meat off the bone and into pieces.

AND . . .

Finding lamb fillets

The fillets on a spit lamb are glorious. During the braai they get flavour from the bone that they're attached to and are basted by fat dripping onto them from the ribs; in addition to that, as is the case with all fillets, they are very tender.

As you know the loin chop of lamb equals the T-bone of beef. It's just considerably smaller, due to the comparative sizes of the animals. So, whereas a beef fillet is a substantial thing weighing on average about 1.5 kg, a lamb fillet is roughly the size of a deboned and skinned chicken breast. When cutting up the rack of loin chops this fillet is sliced into tiny pieces, and you can find it on the one side of the lamb loin chop – that juicy little piece of meat on the one side of the bone, less than a mouthful per chop. When dealing with a whole lamb on a spit, this fillet is obviously not yet cut into pieces and is still there for the taking. Depending on the circumstances, there are two ways of getting hold of the fillet:

a. If you are at a commercial spit braai function, stroll over to the braaier manning the spit and ask him for it. He will probably be bored from tending a dead lamb for the past few hours, will welcome the company, and will cut it out for you when it's ready. If you take this route, it's prudent to arrive at said conversation with an extra drink, just to make sure the guy doing the spit knows where his loyalties lie.

b. If you are at a farmyard or backyard spit, find the other guy there who has read this book and strike an allegiance. Remember, a lamb has two fillets.

Locating the lamb fillet is really easy, if you know where to look. And fortunately, many people don't look there. The fillets of a lamb, as with beef and pork fillets, are located on the 'inside' of the carcass. They lie parallel on both sides of the spine behind the ribs, close to the legs. Those two long inviting pieces of meat running on each side of the outside backbone that everybody goes for, and mistakenly thinks are the fillets, are in fact the 'sirloins' of a lamb.

Chicken

Braaing chicken is one of those things a lot of people are not entirely comfortable with and many consider chicken to be the most difficult of the popular braai meats to master. This is because chicken meat needs to be braaied right through and the parts closest to the bone are frequently not done by the time the skin has already started to burn. But braaing chicken should not be hard and you should think of it like this: compared to beef, lamb and pork, braaing a whole chicken is really pretty straightforward.

When you braai chicken you need to go easy on the marinade. Thick marinades (usually containing sugar) will burn easily so stay away from them. Also avoid marinades with tomato sauce, which quickly turn black and look burnt. Words you are looking for in a marinade are vinegar, lemon juice, wine and even water.

Although not ideal, some types of meat can be braaied even when they are half-frozen. Chicken is not one of them. Never ever braai frozen or half-frozen chicken as you will be fighting a losing battle and you're almost guaranteed a burnt outside and half-raw inside. If you're the designated braaier at some social gathering and someone hands you frozen chicken, it's entirely acceptable to refuse to take it and request that they braai it themselves.

Take it easy on moderate heat and turn the meat often. You're basically trying to recreate the rotisserie chicken effect so observe a rotisserie chicken system next time you see one. Obviously your braaied chicken will taste even better than the rotisserie chicken as it will have everything that one has plus the added flavour of braai.

For a whole flat chicken that takes about 40 minutes to braai you might need to manufacture backup coals. The easiest way to do this is to add new wood to your fire when the fire is half-finished (after about 20 minutes). By the time you start braaing, that new wood will be halfway there. You then scrape some coals that are ready for braaing to the area where you will braai, and leave the rest of the fire to continue burning while you start cooking.

FLAT CHICKEN

Flat or butterflied chicken is a visually appealing meal to prepare and because it takes a while to cook, it gives you plenty of time to stand around the braai.

WHAT YOU NEED (feeds 2-4)

1 whole chicken

ingredients for your choice of sauce as a marinade:

   peri-peri (page 134),
   garlic, lemon and herb (page 72),
   chimichurri (page 138)
   chermoula (page 110)

HOW TO FLATTEN A CHICKEN

1. Remove the chicken from its packaging and check inside the cavity to see if the giblets (innards) were placed there. If so, remove them and throw them away if you don't have another use for them.

2. Place the chicken on a cutting board, breast side down. Now take a sharp meat knife, cleaver or scissors and cut out the backbone by slicing or cutting along the length of it on both sides. The backbone is exactly where you expect it to sit, running all along the middle of the back.

3. Now that the backbone is gone, the chicken will be 'open' but won't be flat yet. Turn it around, so that the opening you just created is on the board and the breasts are on top. Place each of your thumbs on a breast, and use your other fingers to grab around the chicken, break it open and flatten it. Now press on the chicken with the palm of your hand and use your own body weight to complete the flattening process.

4. Cut away and discard any excess fat or skin that you don't like the look of.

5. Lastly, press on the thick parts of the two chicken breasts to guide some meat to the thinner part of the chicken breast, distributing the meat more evenly within the breast cavity.

HOW TO BRAAI A FLAT CHICKEN

1. Flatten the chicken as above.

2. Rub and coat the chicken with your choice of marinade. Bonus points if you gently lift the skin here and there, and get some marinade on the meat under the skin. Cover and leave it in the fridge for a few hours or overnight.

3. Braai over medium heat, turning often, for 39 minutes until the chicken is done and has an internal temperature of 77°C in the thickest parts (no blood left next to the bones). The given time of 39 minutes is obviously an approximation but is usually pretty accurate.

4. During the second half of the braai you can baste the chicken with left-over marinade or some additional sauce of your choice. If you're basting with left-over marinade, don't baste during the last 5 minutes of the braai; otherwise your meat will be contaminated with raw chicken juice.

AND . . .

■ You can buy flat marinated chickens from a supermarket but there are drawbacks. That marinade frequently contains sugar, which will burn before the chicken is ready. Additionally, they are quite expensive as you're paying chicken meat prices for all that marinade in the bag.

■ Odd bits of raw chicken and chicken juices can and will attract salmonella bacteria. Make sure you clean all work areas and implements properly after flattening the chicken to avoid food poisoning.

CHICKEN PIECES, SLICED AND SPICED

The inherent problem when braaing chicken pieces is that the skin and outside can start to burn before the inside next to the bone is cooked properly. By making a deep slice right to the bone of each chicken piece, you allow the heat to get to that bone and cook the chicken from the inside. This slice also brings the marinade and spices as well as the great taste of braai right into the centre of the meat.

In the Cape Town township of Gugulethu is the world-famous Mzoli's Chisa Nyama. On weekend afternoons it gets quite busy behind the braai fires and there isn't always time to braai chicken pieces in the conventional manner. The braaiers speed up the process by employing the same technique as above and slicing each piece to the bone - so if this slicing sounds a bit progressive for you and you're not sure whether to believe me, then trust Mzoli.

WHAT YOU NEED (feeds 6)

12 chicken pieces (drumsticks or thighs)

1 tot soft butter

1 tot chopped garlic

1 tot lemon juice

1 tot chopped fresh herbs (parsley, sage, rosemary, thyme, basil)

1 tsp salt

1 tsp pepper

WHAT TO DO

1. Mix all the ingredients (except for the chicken) together.

2. Take a sharp knife and make a long, deep cut down to the bone on each drumstick and one or two deep cuts in the top of each thigh.

3. Use a teaspoon to place some of the mixture in each cut and use your recently washed hands to rub the mixture into the cuts properly. Rub any remaining marinade all over the chicken pieces.

4. Braai over medium coals for about 20 minutes turning regularly, until done.

AND . . .

Chicken pieces braaied in this manner can also be marinated in peri-peri sauce (page 134) or chermoula (page 110).

HOW TO BRAAI CHICKEN WINGS SUCCESSFULLY

Chicken wings are a great starter. A chicken wing has a lot of skin and you want that skin to be evenly crisp without getting burnt. The bigger the surface area of skin that you expose to the coals, the easier to achieve this goal.

Regarding the sauce, chicken wings taste best in a sweet and sticky sauce – the problem is that marinating them in a sweet and sticky sauce is unfortunately contradictory to getting the skin crisp. If you marinate the wings in a thick sauce you will have difficulty braaing the skin crisp and if you do manage, the sugar in the marinade will blacken before you manage to crisp the skin. So the trick is to not marinate them before you've braaied them crisp. This is how you do it:

WHAT YOU NEED (feeds 4–6)

1 kg–1.5 kg chicken wings (12–18 chicken wings)

½ cup honey or golden syrup

½ cup tomato sauce

1 tot apple juice

½ tot soy sauce

½ tot paprika

WHAT TO DO

1. Make the sweet and sticky sauce: Mix all the ingredients (apart from the chicken) together in a bowl.

2. Prepare the wings: If you have time and want to make the effort, skewer them; if you are lazy, just take hold of each wing at both ends and pull them open a bit.

3. Braai the wings for 20 minutes over medium-to-hot coals until they become crisp and are almost ready. Don't marinate them first, just braai them.

4. Remove the wings from the fire, put them in a bowl and pour the sauce over them. Toss the wings around with a spoon or braai tongs, making sure all of them are coated with sauce.

5. Then it's back to the braai for another 5 minutes until the sauce is glazed and you get a nice sizzle going on the wings.

6. Remove from the braai and serve.

AND . . .

- This meal also lends itself to a bit of extra bite so if you'd like to, add a few chopped chillies or about half a tot of chilli powder when making the sauce.
- Buffalo chicken wings are made by deep-frying chicken wings in oil, a meal infinitely inferior to the feast you will prepare with this recipe.
- If you don't like a sweet and sticky sauce, use the peri-peri sauce (page 134) or the teriyaki sauce (page 136).

HOW TO BRAAI CHICKEN BREASTS AND MAKE CHICKEN BURGERS

The thing to do with chicken breasts is make chicken burgers. Alternatively, slice up the meat post braai and make a chicken Caesar salad (page 88). You obviously need the breasts to be skinned and deboned; these are also known as chicken breast fillets. The typical chicken breast fillet is a bit lopsided with a bulky part and a thin point, so put the breast fillet on a chopping board and give it a few gentle whacks on the thick part with a meat tenderising mallet before the braai. This will make it uniform in thickness, which makes for easier braaing and will soften the meat for biting through when it's on the burger. If you hit it too much, it will disintegrate, and you will be left with chicken mince. You don't want that so do be gentle with the mallet.

This is stating the obvious, but a chicken burger contains meat, salad, dairy and starch, so it really is a balanced meal all on its own.

WHAT YOU NEED (per burger)
1 chicken breast
salt and pepper (or braai salt)
olive oil
1 hamburger roll
2 slices of tomato
1 lettuce leaf
cheese
mayonnaise
peri-peri sauce (page 134)

WHAT TO DO

1. Place each chicken breast fillet flat on a chopping board and lightly pound the thick side with a meat mallet, wine bottle, rolling pin, side of a meat cleaver or any other item of sufficient weight and size. You want the whole fillet more uniform in thickness and this step will make the meat easier to braai, better looking on your burger and softer to bite.

2. Spice each chicken fillet with salt and pepper or your favourite braai salt. Either brush each one with oil or simply pour a bit of oil into the bowl with them and toss the fillets around until all are coated.

3. Braai the meat for about 6–10 minutes until it is done. The nice thing about chicken breast fillets is that you can actually see the meat colour changing from raw to ready on the braai.

4. Assemble the burger: Buttered roll, chicken breast, cheese, peri-peri sauce, mayonnaise, tomato and lettuce leaf. When assembling burgers I always like to place the cheese right next to the patty so that the heat of the meat can melt the cheese.

HOW TO MAKE POTATO WEDGES

Parboil potatoes in salted water until just soft, but not too soft: a fork should just be able to go in – this will take about 20 minutes. Drain very well, i.e. get all the water off. Cut into wedges, toss around in olive oil, and generously sprinkle the wedges with coarse sea salt. Bake in an oven pre-heated to 200°C until brown and crispy – this will take about 25 minutes.

Serve with your chicken burgers.

CHICKEN, FETA AND SUNDRIED TOMATO BURGER PATTIES

All burger patties are not created equal. As far as chicken goes, this one is pretty regal.

WHAT YOU NEED (4 burgers)

4 chicken breasts

2 feta cheese rounds

1 pack sundried tomatoes (200–250 g)

olive oil

salt and pepper

4 hamburger rolls

fresh basil or rocket leaves

tinfoil

WHAT TO DO

1. Cut chicken breasts, feta and sundried tomatoes into pieces.

2. Mix them together in a bowl with salt and pepper and a little olive oil, just enough to make the mixture stick together.

3. Divide the mixture into four, and make four patties.

4. Place a sheet of tinfoil in a hinged grid, and wet the foil in four patches with olive oil. Place the patties on these four spots, and start to braai. The risk of burning is minimal due to the foil, so heat is not your enemy and you can braai on hot to very hot coals.

5. Place another sheet of oiled foil on top of the patties, close the grid, and turn. Continue braaing the patties between the sheets of foil until the chicken is done.

6. Remove the foil and serve on buttered rolls with fresh basil leaves or rocket leaves or both.

AND . . .

This recipe is inspired by Lise Beyers, one of the first journalists to support National Braai Day in print, i.e. I like her. She uses pitted black olives instead of sundried tomato, doesn't tell you to include the fresh leaves on the burger and she braais the patties without the aid of tinfoil. I suggest you try all these options and see what works for you.

THE ROTHERHAMBURGER

The Rotherhamburger is a pretty decadent creation. It's inspired by my friend Seth Rotherham and his philosophy, 'work is a sideline, live the holiday!'

WHAT YOU NEED (makes 4)

4 chicken breast fillets

4 hamburger rolls

salt and pepper
(or your favourite braai salt)

olive oil

8 slices bacon

8 slices salami

8 slices mozzarella cheese

feta cheese (crumbled)

WHAT TO DO

1. Place each chicken breast fillet flat on a chopping board and lightly pound the thick side with a meat mallet, wine bottle, rolling pin, side of a meat cleaver or any other item of sufficient weight and size. You want the whole fillet more uniform in thickness and this step will make the meat easier to braai, better looking on your burger and softer to bite.

2. Spice each chicken fillet with salt and pepper or your favourite braai salt. Either brush each one with the oil or simply pour a bit of oil into the bowl with them and toss the fillets around until they are all coated.

3. Braai the meat for about 6–10 minutes on hot coals until it is done. The nice thing about chicken breast fillets is that you can actually see the meat colour changing from raw to ready on the braai.

4. Fry the bacon while the chicken is braaing. You can do this in a pan on the fire or in a pan on a stove, or alternatively simply braai it on the grid with the chicken.

5. Assemble the burger as follows: salami, feta, chicken breast, mozzarella, bacon. (The chicken and bacon will melt the mozzarella, thus logic dictates that you can also assemble it in this order: bacon, mozzarella, chicken, feta, salami.)

AND . . .

Experiment with the salami you use for this recipe. There is a big variety out there so try things like chorizo or pepperoni to add new and interesting flavour dimensions to your burger.

PORTUGUESE CHICKEN

It's a proven fact that peri-peri braaied chicken is incredibly popular and tastes great. There's even a very successful restaurant chain built on this principle. But your chicken will taste better than their's because you are braaing with wood and they braai with gas. We've now reached the part of this book where you will need to mix a bottle of peri-peri sauce. If you haven't already done so, turn to page 134 now and get cracking.

WHAT YOU NEED (feeds 6)
12 chicken pieces
peri-peri sauce (page 134)

WHAT TO DO

1. Pour the peri-peri sauce over the chicken pieces or throw the chicken pieces into the bowl you made the marinade in and toss them around until they are properly coated. There is no need to use all the sauce you made so take some of it out the bowl first as you can't use it again once you've had raw meat in it. A resealable plastic bag is also a great place for meat and marinade to spend some quality time together.

2. Cover the bowl, put it in the fridge and let the chicken marinate for a few hours or even overnight. If you feel inclined to do so, spoon some of the marinade lying in the bottom of the bowl over the pieces from time to time.

3. Braai the chicken pieces on medium to hot coals for about 20–25 minutes until done. Chicken should have no blood left in it and any juices running free next to the bone should be clear. The skin should be crisp but not burnt (realistically there will be a few black spots of caramelised skin here and there). During the braai, use a brush to paint any leftover marinade or extra peri-peri sauce onto the chicken. Never paint any sauce that has been in contact with raw chicken during the last few minutes of a braai, otherwise your chicken will be contaminated with raw meat juices.

4. If you've already bought your meat thermometer, you might as well check the internal temperature of the thickest parts. If it's 77°C then you know that the chicken is done.

5. Serve the chicken with some extra peri-peri sauce on the side.

AND . . .

If you think that not enough marinade will penetrate the meat, then make a stylish cut to the bone of each chicken piece as explained in the 'Chicken pieces, sliced and spiced' recipe on page 72. This cut will also speed up the braaing process.

CHICKEN ROASTED IN THE MAN-OVEN

This recipe is so easy that I almost didn't put it in the book. But I get asked about it a lot, so here it is. Read more about Man-Ovens on page 197.

WHAT YOU NEED (feeds 4)

1 chicken

1-2 tots of your favourite chicken spice or rub

1 can of cider, ginger beer, beer, coke, apple juice or grape juice

4-8 medium to large potatoes

WHAT TO DO

1. Open the chosen can of soda/cider/beer/juice and throw a third of the contents down your throat. Now let the remaining contents in the can reach room temperature. (A can at room temperature is better than an ice-cold can as the liquid will steam sooner.) If you feel like it and have an old-style tin opener, make a few additional holes in the top part of the can. Alternatively use some part of your multi-tool to make those holes but be careful not to injure yourself.

2. Light the charcoal fire and set up your Man-Oven for indirect grilling. In a Kamado-style oven this means using the deflector plate; in a kettle braai this means having two heaps of coals on the sides of the bottom grid and leaving the middle of the bottom grid open.

3. If relevant, ensure that you remove the little bag of giblets from the cavity of the chicken.

4. Rub the chicken inside and out with the braai spice.

5. Push the can prepared in step 1 into the cavity of the chicken.

6. Place the chicken standing upright (with the can inside also facing upright) into the middle of the top grid of your Man-Oven and pack the potatoes around it.

7. Close the lid of the Man-Oven and bake the chicken for 1 hour at 180°C. Make sure that the bottom and top air vents are open, otherwise the coals will smother and die.

8. Do not open the lid for the next 50 minutes.

9. After 50 minutes to 1 hour the chicken will be ready. The skin will be crisp and some of the liquid from the can will have steamed into the chicken making the meat moist and also giving it more flavour. Chicken is done when its internal temperature is 77°C on your meat thermometer.

10. Remove the chicken from the Man-Oven, discard the can and its leftover liquid, and let the chicken rest for a few minutes before carving it.

11. Serve with the potatoes, which will by now have crisp skins and be completely soft inside.

CHICKEN CURRY *POTJIE*

I really love chicken curry, and there came a time in my life when it was simply too expensive to go to a restaurant every time I had a craving for it. Fortunately it's quite simple to make yourself. A valuable skill then, that's easy to master.

WHAT YOU NEED (feeds 4)

8-12 chicken pieces (use legs, thighs or breasts; no wings, braai them for starters)

1 large onion (chopped)

oil (either olive or sunflower)

5 garlic cloves (chopped or crushed)

diced fresh ginger
(equal quantity to garlic)

1-2 tots masala curry mix*

1 tin chopped tomatoes

6 potatoes (peeled and in chunks)

salt and pepper

6 carrots (peeled and in chunks)

2 tots tomato paste

1 cup fresh cream
(or coconut cream or plain yoghurt)

honey

WHAT TO DO

1. Fry the chopped onion in some oil in a *potjie* over high heat for about 4 minutes until it is golden and then add the garlic, ginger and masala curry mix. After another minute add the chicken pieces and fry them until golden brown. (Remember to position the pot on the flames of the fire to do the frying part of any *potjie*. After that move the pot to another area where you just place a few coals under the pot to keep it at a gentle simmer.)

2. Add a little water and stir the chicken pieces a bit, ensuring none of them are sticking to the bottom of the pot as this will cause them to burn. Add the tin of tomatoes as well as the potatoes. Grind salt and pepper onto the food.

3. Put the lid on the pot and then adjust the heat of the pot to a gentle simmer by moving either the pot or the coals of the fire.

4. After 45 minutes remove the lid and toss in the carrots. Check on the moisture level of the pot and add a little bit of water if it looks too dry. Replace the lid.

5. After another 45 minutes add the tomato paste and cream, yoghurt or coconut cream.

6. Wait for 5 minutes and then start tasting the food.

a. Add more salt if it needs it, and if it needs to be sweeter, add honey.
b. If at this stage the curry is too strong, add more cream, coconut cream or plain yoghurt to it and if you want more burn, add more masala or chilli powder.

c. If there is too much water in the pot then let it simmer without the lid until it has reduced adequately.

7. As soon as you like the taste and amount of liquid in the *potjie*, the food is ready to serve. Total cooking time should be about 2 hours. Serve with basmati rice or pieces of fresh bread.

*Masala is a mixture of the spices needed to make a curry. Go to a spice market and tell them what you intend to cook. They will mix one for you or sell you a pre-mixed packet. Alternatively start by simply buying off-the-shelf masala at a supermarket. Not all masalas are equal in ferocity and the strength depends on the ratios of ingredients. Two typical ingredients, chilli powder and paprika powder, look about the same but the one has a lot of burn and the other is pretty harmless. Ask advice from the person behind the counter.

CHICKEN CAESAR SALAD

You can serve the chicken Caesar salad as a main meal. The Caesar is one of the world's classic salads and the great thing about it is that you can braai but still only eat a salad - the ultimate loophole.

WHAT YOU NEED

(feeds 4 as a main meal)

4 chicken breasts

1 head romaine lettuce (torn apart and washed; if you cannot find one use normal lettuce)

2 cups white bread
(cubed in 1 × 1 cm blocks)

5 tots olive oil

3 cloves garlic (crushed or chopped)

1 egg

2 tots red wine vinegar

1 lemon (juiced)

1 tsp Worcestershire sauce

1 tsp mustard

3 anchovy fillets (optional, if you don't like anchovy leave it out)

1 tsp capers, drained (optional)

salt and pepper

3 tots Parmesan cheese
(grated or shaved)

WHAT TO DO

1. Make the croutons: Slice the bread into 1 × 1 cm blocks. Mix 2 crushed garlic cloves with 2 tots of olive oil and mix that with the bread. Spread on an oven baking-tray and bake at 180°C for 10 minutes until golden brown.

2. Make the dressing: Boil the egg for 1 minute, no longer. Remove from the water and let it cool off. This is called 'coddling'. Now mix the remaining crushed clove of garlic, the vinegar, lemon juice, Worcestershire sauce, mustard, anchovies and capers. Whisk everything together and then add the egg. Whisk again. Now slowly, and bit by bit, while you are continuously whisking, add the remaining 3 tots of olive oil. At the end of this add salt and pepper to taste.

3. Braai the chicken breasts: Braai the four chicken breasts over high heat until done. Remove from the fire, let them rest a few minutes and slice. For a more comprehensive description on how to braai chicken breasts, turn to 'How to braai chicken breasts and make chicken burgers' on page 76.

4. Assemble the salad: Add the lettuce leaves, croutons and half of the dressing to a bowl and toss. Top with the chicken pieces and Parmesan cheese. Serve with remaining dressing on the side.

AND . . .

There is some half-raw egg in the sauce so first, don't mention it to your guests, and second, eat the salad on the day you make it. Alternatively, just leave the egg out of the recipe.

THE BEST CHICKEN TIKKA MASALA

Chicken tikka masala is one of the most famous meals to come from a tandoori oven, which is a cylindrical clay oven heated by a fire, almost like a braai. Tikka means 'pieces' but chicken tikka refers to a specific meal of chicken pieces marinated in a masala spice and yoghurt, skewered and cooked in a tandoori (or, in this case, braaied). Chicken tikka masala is one of my all-time favourite curries – and sure to be one of your's once you've nailed this recipe.

WHAT YOU NEED (feeds 4)

The chicken
600 g deboned, skinless chicken meat (a pack of 4 chicken breasts)

1 cup plain yoghurt

2 tots chicken tikka masala spice
(or tandoori masala or any good masala mix that is red in colour that you can find at your local spice market)

1 tot lemon juice

about 6 skewers

The sauce
1 tot garlic

1 tot ginger

oil or butter

1 × 400 g can tomato purée
(or chopped tomatoes)

2-3 tots tomato paste

1 cup cream

½ cup coconut cream

1 tsp garam masala (This tastes different from and is slightly hotter than normal masala as it contains different ingredients and ratios of ingredients. You need to trust me that this is the masala you need for the dish so go find it at a spice market.)

1 tsp turmeric powder

1 tsp paprika

½ tsp chilli powder
(optional, can be less or more)

2 tots ground almonds

salt

honey

2 tots chopped coriander leaves
(dhania)

WHAT TO DO

1. Cut the chicken into bite-size chunks and mix in a marinating bowl with the yoghurt, masala spice and lemon juice. Cover and leave in the fridge to marinate for a few hours or overnight.

2. Skewer the chicken pieces (make sosaties) and braai over hot coals until done. Don't worry about the odd black spot of caramelised chicken appearing.

3. In a cast-iron pot or fireproof pan lightly fry the garlic and ginger in a bit of oil or butter. If there is any leftover marinade, also add this.

4. After 2 minutes add all the other ingredients except for the salt, honey and coriander leaves. Simmer the sauce for 15 minutes. While it is simmering, look at the sauce and taste it. If you want to, make the following adjustments:

- Add salt if it needs more.
- Make the sauce hotter by adding more chilli powder and/or sweeter by adding honey.
- To make the colour of the sauce redder add extra paprika or to make it more yellow or orange add extra turmeric.

5. When the sauce is to your liking, starts to thicken, and the chicken is braaied, remove the skewers and add the sauce to the chicken pieces. Stir in the dhania or coriander leaves and serve with basmati rice.

AND . . .

If you reckon you can multi-task then you can obviously braai the chicken and cook the sauce concurrently.

Boerewors

- -

Boerewors is a true Rainbow Nation creation – a culmination of local culinary skills with those from the European and Eastern arrivals. Sausage-making skills from the Europeans, spices and the knowledge of how to use them from the East, and good South African meat, fire and braai knowhow from the locals all combined to produce this unique braai classic.

There are literally thousands of options out there and no hard-and-fast rule on how to know whether a particular wors will be good. Names like Grabouw or Plaaswors mean very little. Every butcher makes his own version and makes his own decision regarding what meat goes into his boerewors. Some supermarket chains have central distribution points for meat but often the wors gets made on site and so will differ from one store to the next.

The solution is: Get to know your butcher. Even supermarkets have butchers so whether you buy your meat from an independent butcher or at a supermarket, talk to the person who makes the wors and if you don't like him or his wors, shop around until you find a place that works for you. You will eventually find a winner, whether he operates independently or in a supermarket.

Boerewors is usually made with a combination of beef and pork, or just beef. The bulk of that will be meat, but some of it will be fat. A typical boerewors can, for example, have a 70:30 beef-to-pork mix with a meat-to-fat ratio of 80:20. A good boerewors comes in a natural casing. These are cleaned and sanitised sheep or pork intestines. In general the thinner ones are from sheep and the thicker ones from pork.

A good butcher should be able to tell you what meats are in the wors, i.e. his beef-to-pork ratio and his meat-to-fat ratio. The spices might be a branded premix or could be his personal in-house recipe. In the latter case that part of the recipe will probably be a secret but he should still be able to tell you what meat he uses.

Remember, if it does not say 'boerewors' on the packaging then it is not boerewors, even if it looks like boerewors. The biggest culprit here is the inferior 'braaiwors', which could contain various other things apart from meat. My advice is to stay away from 'braaiwors' if your pocket allows and stick to 'boerewors'. From there on you will simply have to shop around until you find a butcher and product that you trust and like.

Perfectly braaied boerewors has an internal temperature of 71°C. Before that it is still raw and after that you are drying it out.

BOEREWORS ROLLS WITH TOMATO-CHILLI RELISH

The most important thing about boerewors rolls is the boerewors. In classic terms a boerewors roll is made by putting a piece of braaied boerewors in a hotdog roll with a topping of either tomato sauce or chutney. This recipe takes it a bit further.

WHAT YOU NEED

(10 boerewors rolls)

1 kg of your favourite boerewors

10 hot dog rolls

tomato relish (see below)

WHAT YOU NEED FOR TOMATO-CHILLI RELISH

1 tin peeled and chopped tomatoes (or 2 cups chopped fresh tomatoes, peeled or unpeeled)

1 onion (finely chopped)

1 red pepper (finely chopped)

oil or butter

just less than 1 tsp chilli powder

2 cloves garlic (crushed or chopped)

1 tot tomato paste

1 tot chutney

1 tot balsamic vinegar (This is the only time in the book I think balsamic vinegar is the best for a recipe, but if you don't feel like buying it, use normal vinegar and add a bit more sugar to the relish according to your taste. While on the topic, you should actually be adding sugar and salt to any recipe according to your taste.)

1 tot sugar

1 tsp salt

WHAT TO DO

1. Before you braai the wors, make the relish (see below).

2. Now it is time to braai the wors. The aim is to break or pierce it as little as possible and have as juicy an end product as possible.

a. Do not pre-cut the wors as its juices will get lost. Keep it long and coil it, or position it on the grid running back and forth like an airport queue.

b. The easiest method is to braai the boerewors in a hinged grid so that it can be turned without breaking. Failing that, coil it and, while it is on a flat surface, press two skewers all the way through the wors at a 90 degree angle to each other, effectively putting the wors in a little skewer cross. In this way you can braai and turn the wors easily on an open grid without it breaking apart and losing juices.

c. Boerewors can be braaied on any type of heat – the braai times will just differ. I prefer fairly hot coals so the skin is crisp and snaps under your teeth while the insides are still nice and juicy. Depending on heat and wors thickness, braai time should be somewhere between 5 and 10 minutes, and you should turn it between one and five times. On pathetic third round coals (when you are last in line at the bring-and-braai) braai time can be 20 minutes and the wors will still taste fine but this should be the exception and not the norm.

d. Do not 'pop' the wors and let the juices escape. Most of that stuff is meat juice, not fat. If you feel the wors is too fatty then buy better wors from a better butcher in future.

e. Do not over-braai it. If you braai it too long it will become dry and you will kill some of the flavour. I have never been served boerewors that I thought would have benefited from being braaied longer. 71°C is perfect.

3. When the wors is ready the skin will be brown in most parts and grey in some. Place a piece of wors in each hotdog roll and pour a few spoons of relish over it.

WHAT TO DO FOR TOMATO-CHILLI RELISH

1. Go and light your fire. Using a pan or pot on the fire or stove, fry the onion and pepper in a bit of oil or butter for 5 minutes. Add the chilli and garlic and fry for 1 more minute.

2. Now add the tomatoes, tomato paste, chutney, vinegar, sugar and salt, and mix well.

3. As soon as the mixture starts to boil, turn the heat down by either moving the pan to the edge of the fire or turning the stove to low so that it's just simmering. By the time you've finished braaing, the flavours of your relish will have developed nicely. At some stage while you're waiting for the fire to burn out, check up on the relish. If you want it to be sweeter, add more sugar and if you want more kick, add extra chilli powder.

Seafood

The first rule of braaing seafood is to braai only fresh seafood and there is really no substitute for this rule.

There are some ways to check whether fish is fresh like looking at it (must have bright eyes and shiny skin), pressing on the flesh and seeing whether it bounces back (if the dent stays, the fish is probably old) or smelling it (if it smells like old fish, it is) but in my experience the best ways to get hold of fresh fish are:

- Catch it yourself.
- Buy it fresh from fishermen on a beach or at a harbour.
- Buy it from a fishmonger that you trust.

Shellfish like prawns that were frozen immediately after they were caught can be successfully braaied and reputable fishmongers usually have a great selection of frozen prawns. Some people allege that crayfish can be frozen and then braaied at a later date as well but I have no idea whether this is true; I like crayfish too much and inevitably consume all of it on the day that it comes into my possession.

Any fresh fish braaied with a basting of butter, garlic, lemon juice, parsley, salt and pepper will taste great. No fish has ever complained when white wine was also added to this basic recipe. If you'd like a bit of bite add some chilli or paprika, and for a savoury taste add some soy sauce. Always rub or paint the fish with oil before the braai so that it doesn't stick to the grid.

There are generally three ways to braai fish: whole and closed, whole and open, or as fillets. All three are explained in this chapter. In each case you can also wrap the fish in foil, which significantly decreases the chances that you will burn it, and means that you can braai it over higher heat. The fish will steam which isn't necessarily a bad thing but it will have much less of a braai fire flavour, which *is* a bad thing.

Some people like to cut the fish into thick slices, as you would slice bread, and they call them 'fish steaks'. By slicing through the fish like this you are cutting the bones into pieces and exponentially increase the chances that a piece of fishbone will get stuck in your throat. I will not discuss this method of braaing fish further except to strongly advise against it.

FISH ON THE BRAAI IS READY:

- when it flakes when you insert a knife or fork,
- if it comes away from the bones when you pull the flesh,
- when the meat changes from translucent to white,
- but the most foolproof way, which holds true for more than 9 out of every 10 braais, is that by the time you think it's ready it probably is.

HOW TO BRAAI A WHOLE FISH, OPEN

When you braai an absolutely fresh fish properly, it's guaranteed to be a great meal, an anchor in a world of uncertainty. I cannot stress enough how important it is that the fish you braai is fresh. Now as mentioned before, you can either braai a whole fish 'open' or 'closed' and the choice is really a matter of personal preference. Braaing the fish open exposes a larger area of the fish to direct heat and braai flavour, and is also quicker.

The crucial piece of equipment for this recipe is a hinged grid (*toeklaprooster*) and attempting to turn the fish without one is silly.

Fish like Cape salmon, cod and yellowtail are popular on the braai but there are many other types of fish you can also braai so ask the fishmonger's advice and try to ensure the fish you buy is not on an endangered list. Ask for your fish to be gutted and scaled and for its head to be removed. If you caught the fish yourself then I assume you know how to do that.

WHAT YOU NEED

(1.5 kg fish feeds about 4,
2 kg fish feeds 6)
1 whole fresh fish (something like Cape salmon, cod or yellowtail)
½ cup butter (melted)
4 cloves garlic (chopped)
juice of 2 lemons
1 tot chopped parsley
olive or sunflower oil
salt and pepper

WHAT TO DO

1. Melt the butter and mix in the garlic, lemon juice and parsley. You will use this sauce to baste the fish while it is braaing.

2. An 'open' fish has two sides, a flesh side and a skin side. Rub or paint the oil onto both sides and then grind salt and pepper onto the flesh side only.

3. Place fish in a hinged grid and braai it on medium to hot coals, flesh side down, for about 3–4 minutes until the flesh gets a light golden colour. Now turn the grid over and braai the fish skin side down until done. Total braai time should be between 14 and 20 minutes depending on the size of the fish, the height of grid and the heat of the fire. Baste throughout with your sauce made from the melted butter, lemon juice, parsley and garlic. Although you should try and keep it to a minimum, don't worry if the skin side burns slightly here and there – you're not going to eat the skin. I treat fish skin at the braai as a natural tinfoil.

4. The fish is ready when it has turned white, comes away from the bones when you try to loosen it or flakes when you insert a fork into it. Remember the golden rule: If you think it's ready, it probably is.

AND . . .

A slightly smaller fish, say about 1.3 kg whole, with its head and tail subsequently removed, fits very nicely onto a standard-sized hinged grid together with four crayfish halves. All of this can be braaied together for 14 minutes and makes a feast for four people.

HOW TO BRAAI A WHOLE FISH, CLOSED

You can use a special fish-shaped hinged grid for this braai, but a big enough normal hinged grid will also do the job. It takes me about 30 and my father about 40 minutes to braai a fish like this. He's a much more relaxed braaier than I am, and calls me an 'aggressive braaier' (on average I use four more pieces of wood than him per fire).

We like to make a few slashes into both sides of the fish to allow the marinade and heat to penetrate better.

WHAT YOU NEED

(1.5 kg fish feeds about 4,
2 kg fish feeds about 6)

1 fresh fish (gutted and scaled but with head and tail intact. Cape salmon, cod and yellowtail are popular braai fish but there are many other types of fish you can also braai so ask the fishmonger's advice and try to ensure the fish you buy is not on an endangered list)

olive or sunflower oil

salt and pepper

1 tot chopped parsley

4 or more cloves garlic
(crushed or chopped)

½ cup butter (melted)

juice of 2 lemons

WHAT TO DO

1. Make about four diagonal slashes in the flesh on each side of the fish. This gives the heat and flavour better access.

2. Rub or paint the outside of the fish with oil and then grind salt and black pepper all over the outside and inside of the fish. Rub half of the parsley and garlic into the slashes and sprinkle the other half inside the cavity of the fish. If you like garlic, use more.

3. Mix the butter and lemon juice and put some of that into the cavity of the fish.

4. Now put the fish in the hinged grid and braai over gentle heat for 30 to 40 minutes until ready. Baste the fish with the rest of the butter and lemon juice sauce. When you turn the fish, do it gently. If you run out of sauce make more, or bulk it up by adding white wine.

5. The fish is ready when it has turned white, comes away from the bones when you try to loosen it or flakes when you insert a fork into it. Remember the golden rule: If you think it's ready, it probably is.

AND . . .

■ Every so often you come across a herb garden with fennel growing in it. Should that be the case, take a fresh piece and place it inside the cavity of the fish during the braai.

■ For a bit of burn, add a chopped chilli to the basting sauce.

HOW TO BRAAI SNOEK

Once you have mastered the recipe I give you here, it stands to reason that you will experiment and develop your own special way of braaing snoek, using this as a foundation.

WHAT YOU NEED (feeds 4–6)

1 fresh snoek (when you buy your snoek, ask for it to be cleaned and for the head and tail to be cut off)

4 chopped garlic cloves

½ cup butter or olive oil

½ cup apricot jam

juice of 2 lemons

olive oil

salt and pepper

1 tot soy sauce (optional)

2–4 tots white wine (optional)

dash of chilli sauce (optional)

WHAT TO DO

1. When starting the snoek braai process, wash the snoek under cold running water.

2. Now you need to dry the snoek. Do it in one of three ways:

- Hang it in a cool area with a draught blowing over it. The easiest way to do that is to put it in the hinged grid you will be braaing it in and hang that grid on a hook under a tree.
- Salt the snoek with coarse sea salt that will absorb all the water.
- Blot it with paper kitchen towel.

Whichever of these methods you use, do make sure that your snoek has

some defence system against aerial attack by flies.

3. Using a small pot on the fire or on a stove, lightly fry the chopped garlic in the butter or oil. Then add the apricot jam and lemon juice. If you want to add some of the optional ingredients, do so now. Heat and stir until everything is melted and mixed.

4. If you salted the snoek in step 2, you now have to shake off all the coarse sea salt. Most of the big visible pieces will be shaken off but obviously some of the salt would have transferred onto the snoek so keep this in mind when adding extra salt in one of the next steps. This 'pre-salting' of snoek with coarse sea salt is loved by some, but not by all. You need to test whether it works for you.

5. A snoek should be braaied 'open'. Smear the skin side of the snoek with oil so that it does not stick to the grid and then place it on the grid, skin side down. Grind salt and pepper onto the flesh side of the snoek and lightly pat it onto the meat.

6. There are two ways of braaing the snoek:

- Straight onto the grid. Coals will need to be slightly gentler as the skin might burn more easily on the direct heat. You definitely need to pay more attention in this method and make sure you don't burn the fish. The skin side of the fish will end up slightly crisper and might be charred here and there, but you're not going to eat that skin anyway.
- Foil on grid and fish on foil. Your coals can be hotter in this method as the foil protects the fish from

getting burnt. Another advantage of doing it on foil is that you can fold up the sides of the foil, which saves any basting and sauce that runs off the fish. Fish braaied on foil is also easier to lift onto a serving tray without breaking.

7. Braai time: Whether you are using foil or whether the skin side went straight onto the grid, a snoek should be braaied for about 15 minutes in total. You can deviate slightly from this time depending on the heat of the coals, height of the grid and size of the snoek. Test whether the snoek is ready by inserting a fork in the thickest part and turning the fork slightly. As soon as the flesh flakes, the snoek is ready.

- When braaing without tinfoil I braai for 3 minutes flesh side down and then the rest of the time with the skin side down.
- When braaing with foil I braai for 9 minutes skin side down, 3 minutes flesh side down (and during this time remove the foil from the skin side) and then a final 3 minutes skin side down to brown the skin.

8. Basting the snoek: Baste only when the flesh side is facing up. Use a brush or simply drip it onto the fish with a spoon. You can baste as often as you wish until all the basting is used. Should you find that you'd like to use more basting, then make more sauce next time.

(continued)

HOW TO BRAAI SNOEK (CONTINUED)

AND . . .

- There is always a risk that the fish will stick to the grid, so gently shake whichever side of the grid is on top at any stage of the braai to loosen it from the meat.
- Serve the snoek skin side down, flesh side up.
- Dish up the snoek using a spatula or similar implement.

- Break rather than cut the snoek as cutting also cuts the bones into smaller pieces, which can get stuck in your throat. Normal snoek bones are quite large and you will find them easily.
- Snoek is best served with a side of *soetpatat* (see below).

SOETPATAT

A bit of background on the *soetpatat*. In Afrikaans, my first language and the most commonly spoken language up the West Coast, sweet potato is called *patat*. When slices of *patat* are fried and stewed with butter, sugar and a bit of cinnamon we call it *soetpatat,* which translates to 'sweet sweet potato'. It's an outstanding dish that goes very well with braaied seafood and is the classic side dish to serve with braaied snoek, hence its position in this book - *soetpatat* is not fish, but needs to be served with it.

WHAT YOU NEED (feeds 4-6)

1 cup honey (or sugar)

½ cup butter

1 cinnamon stick

peel of a quarter of an orange

1 kg sweet potato
(peeled and sliced or cut into chunks)

1 tsp salt

WHAT TO DO

1. Melt the honey (or sugar) and butter in a pot. Mix well and when it is all melted, add the cinnamon stick, orange peel, salt and sweet potato slices or chunks.

2. Stir and mix it all together and then put the lid on the pot. Gently simmer with the lid on for about 30 minutes until all the sweet potatoes are soft. During this time you can use a large spoon or spatula to toss the mixture very gently once or twice. Do not remove the lid at any other stage and do not stir more often. Creating mash will taste the same but is not considered stylish.

3. Serve with braaied snoek or any other braaied food for that matter.

CRAYFISH WITH GARLIC-LEMON BUTTER

Whether bought or caught, the crayfish should still be alive when you get hold of it. When fresh, a braaied crayfish tastes incredible and is always tender. The tough thing about crayfish is getting hold of them.

WHAT YOU NEED (feeds 4)

4 whole crayfish (fresh)
½ cup butter
2 garlic cloves (crushed or chopped)
juice of 1 lemon
½ tsp salt
½ tsp pepper

WHAT TO DO

1. Kill the crayfish by inserting a knife between its eyes.

2. Prepare the garlic lemon butter by mixing all the ingredients except the crayfish together. During the braai you can either add dollops of butter to the crayfish using a spoon or knife, or alternatively you can melt the mixture and use a spoon or brush to paint it on.

3. On a cutting board and using a big sharp knife, cut each crayfish in half lengthways and remove the vein running along the length of the tail. If the vein ruptures during this process, wash the crayfish under cold running water and pat it dry with kitchen paper towels.

4. Braai flesh side down for 3–4 minutes on hot coals and then turn them over. Now start basting the flesh with the garlic-and-lemon butter sauce. Braai shell side down for another 7–10 minutes. You are aiming for 10–14 minutes in total. Add the butter mixture to the crayfish only after you have turned them with the flesh facing upwards so that the sauce will be saved and retained by the shell and not all go to waste on the coals. You won't need to add any additional sauces to alter the taste of the end result. The meal is perfect as is.

5. The crayfish are ready to eat when all the flesh has turned white and the tail flesh pulls free from the shell when you lift it with a fork – make sure to hold on to the crayfish with the other hand (or with braai tongs). Don't fiddle with the crayfish while it is braaing. They will not stick to the grid and they are best left alone.

AND . . .

■ You could also steam the crayfish first and then give them a braai flavour on the fire. If you want to try this, steam them for between 5 and 10 minutes and then start from step 2 and braai them as described above but only for the remaining part of the original 14 minutes.

■ Some people have the horrible habit of serving crayfish with a sauce made by mixing tomato sauce and commercial mayonnaise. They usually call this sauce 1000 Island sauce. It has a strong taste and completely overpowers the delicate and lovely flavour of crayfish. You might as well eat a piece of chicken breast because you won't taste the difference. You will notice that there isn't a recipe for that sauce in this book.

PERI-PERI PRAWNS

Braaied prawns are very popular. The fire makes the shells nice and crisp while giving the meat a caramelised and smoky flavour. When braaing prawns it's not important that they be shelled but they do have to be deveined. The shells give flavour and keep them from drying out. Prawns are widely available in South Africa but usually sold frozen. Defrost by leaving them in a bucket or bowl of cold water for 30 minutes. During the braai you preferably want the prawns exposed to direct heat from the coals, so either skewer them and place those skewers in a hinged grid or braai them in a pan with holes in it. Prawns only need to be turned once during the braai, and don't worry if the shells get charred here and there as you can peel them off.

WHAT YOU NEED (feeds 2–4)

1 kg prawns (deveined but preferably in shell and with heads)

peri-peri sauce (see page 134 – you need half the quantity for this prawn recipe so either halve the sauce ingredients or make the whole lot and keep the rest in the fridge for some other awesome meal)

1 tot chopped parsley

WHAT TO DO

1. Thaw the prawns by putting them in a bowl of cold water for 30 minutes.

2. Devein the prawns: Cut open the back of each tail with kitchen scissors starting at the gap between the head and the tail, and then pull out the whole vein using the tine of a fork. This is not a particularly tough job, but takes a while to complete for 1 kg of prawns. Your fishmonger will probably do it for you at a minimal charge so don't be shy to ask.

3. Prepare the peri-peri sauce (see page 134) by stirring all the ingredients together then adding the parsley.

4. Drain the prawns and then drizzle the marinade over them and toss, ensuring all the prawns are coated with sauce. Chucking the prawns and marinade into a plastic bag and sealing it is also an easy way to do it. Let them marinate for 30 minutes to 1 hour.

5. To give the prawns direct exposure to the coals, braai them in a pan with holes in the bottom, a braai basket or on skewers. The prawns are ready after about 6 minutes on medium to hot coals; you will see they are done when the shells change colour from white to pink and the flesh from glassy to opaque.

6. During the 6-minute braai, boil the marinade that is left over in the bowl or bag you used to marinate the prawns in. It's very important that any sauce used as a marinade should be boiled before using it as a dipping sauce.

7. When the prawns are ready, remove from the fire, pour the hot boiled sauce over them and serve immediately. Alternatively, you can discard the marinade and serve the prawns with fresh peri-peri sauce.

AND . . .

- You can also braai the prawns in a normal fireproof, paella-type pan. In that case just throw the prawns and all the marinade into the pan and fry over high heat (lots of coals or even flames) for 6 minutes.
- If you don't like peri-peri prawns then use the garlic, lemon and butter sauce described in the crayfish recipe on page 106.
- There is a photograph of a 'braai pan' with holes in it. Buy yourself one, it works really well for prawns.

WHITE FISH FILLETS IN MOROCCAN CHERMOULA MARINADE

White fish fillets can be a bit bland but this recipe from North Africa will solve that problem. A fragrant combination of herbs and spices results in a dish that is very aromatic yet does not burn the mouths of sensitive eaters. The other great thing about this recipe is that although it's a foreign invention you can prepare it entirely from ingredients that are widely available locally.

WHAT YOU NEED (feeds 6)

6 portions fresh fish fillets
(stay away from hake, it's too soft for the braai)

½ cup olive oil

juice of 1 lemon

2 tots chopped coriander

2 tots chopped parsley

3 garlic cloves (crushed or chopped)

½ tot paprika

1 tsp cumin powder

1 tsp coriander powder

1 tsp salt

WHAT TO DO

1. Make the marinade in a suitable bowl by mixing all the ingredients together (except the fish!) and then either pour it over the fish or put the fish in the bowl you mixed the marinade in. Ensure that all the sides of each fish fillet are coated with marinade.

2. Leave them to marinate for 1 hour.

3. Place the fish in a hinged grid and braai for 8–12 minutes on medium to hot coals until done. Only turn once as the fish fillets will easily flake and break. Take care not to overbraai as fish fillets can dry out quickly.

AND . . .

■ This marinade also goes very well with chicken. Use the marinade above along with the preparation and braai method explained in the 'Chicken pieces, sliced and spiced' recipe on page 72.

■ The other very simple way to braai white fish fillets is in a packet made of tinfoil (or banana leaves if you want to be fancy). Put each fillet on a piece of foil, add a dash of olive oil, squeeze of lemon juice and sprinkle of salt, pepper, garlic and chopped parsley. Close the packet and braai for about 10 minutes on high heat, turning once. Place one packet on each person's plate. Impressive-smelling steam will escape as the packets are opened.

MUSSELS IN A WHITE WINE AND GARLIC SAUCE

Fresh black mussels prepared according to the recipe below is one of the simplest yet most delicious and impressive meals out there. Buy yourself a fishing permit and go collect some mussels during low tide next time you're at the coast. Remember to wear an old pair of shoes otherwise the rocks will cut your feet. Also check with the locals that it's not red tide, as you cannot eat mussels during that time.

WHAT YOU NEED (feeds 4)

1 kg fresh black mussels in shells
1 onion (chopped)
oil or butter
2 cloves garlic
1 cup white wine
1 tsp salt
1 tsp pepper
1 tot parsley
2 tots cream

WHAT TO DO

1. Clean the mussels by scrubbing them with a brush. Remove the beard by pulling it towards the narrow tip of the mussel until it breaks out.

2. Rinse the mussels thoroughly by leaving them in a bucket of fresh water for an hour. Stir the mussels once or twice during this hour so that they all have generous exposure to the fresh water. If there is a lot of sand at the bottom of the bucket, replace the water. At the end of the hour wash the mussels again in clean water. Discard all mussels that are open, floating or have cracked shells. Remember, sand is your enemy. Leaving them in fresh water for 2 hours is even better.

3. In a cast-iron pot, gently fry the onion in a bit of oil or butter. As the onion goes transparent (after about 4 minutes) add the garlic and after another minute add the wine, salt, pepper and, most importantly, the mussels.

4. Place a lid on the pot and let them cook until the shells open. This can happen after 5 minutes and should not take longer than 10 minutes. You can lift the lid occasionally and check on the mussels. As soon as the shells are open the mussels are ready to eat. Discard any mussels that did not open. The white foam in the pot is caused by the proteins in the mussels and is perfectly normal.

5. Add the parsley and cream and toss the mussels to get all of them in contact with the sauce.

6. Serve with pieces of baguette to mop up the sauce. You can also use the empty shells as spoons to eat the sauce with.

7. This meal is a perfect starter as it can be prepared on the flames while you wait for the fire to burn out and form coals for your braai.

AND . . .

■ Adding 250 g of freshly boiled pasta (like spaghetti) to the dish, just as it's ready (after step 5) and stirring it through will give you a very impressive looking and tasting black mussel pasta.
■ For something different, instead of just onion, use onions, carrots and celery in a 2:1:1 ratio.
■ Depending on their size, there are between 40 and 70 mussels in a kilogram and about 30% of that weight is meat.

BRAAIED SALMON WITH WASABI MASHED POTATO

Oslo is the capital of Norway and the Nobel Peace Centre is stationed there. That's the organisation which gave South Africans Albert Luthuli, Desmond Tutu (patron of National Braai Day), Nelson Mandela and FW de Klerk their Nobel Peace Prizes so I went there to check it out. Apart from the Peace Centre the most exciting part of the visit was the potential access to fresh Norwegian salmon and I was not disappointed. Due to the bad weather, I couldn't braai the first piece of fresh fish that I got so I cut it up into pieces and ate a man-sized portion of salmon sashimi. The next day I had better luck with the weather, and managed the braai described below.

WHAT YOU NEED (feeds 4)

4 × 150–200 g fresh Norwegian salmon fillets

2 tots soy sauce

2 tots lemon juice

2 tots olive oil

WHAT TO DO

1. First, light the fire; fish cannot lie in lemon juice marinade for too long.

2. Mix the marinade ingredients in a bowl and add the fish fillets. Let them marinate for about 20 minutes while you wait for the fire to burn out. During this time, use a spoon to scoop marinade onto the exposed parts of the salmon, or flip the fillets over.

3. Braai for about 4 minutes on each side over hot coals until crisp on the outside and still pink on the inside. Fish flakes and breaks easily so you want to handle the fish as little as possible while it's on the grid; it is best to turn it only once.

- The skin will be a bit charred. This is normal and no problem; you don't eat salmon skin.
- I like my salmon still nice and pink in the middle but if you want the fish braaied all the way through go for 5 or 6 minutes per side.

4. Eat immediately while still warm. Serve the salmon on a bed of wasabi-flavoured mashed potato.

5. During the braai, boil any leftover marinade in a pot or pan and spoon a bit of that over each piece of fish as a dressing.

WHAT TO DO FOR WASABI MASHED POTATO

1. Wash 6 medium to large potatoes, then boil them in salted water until very soft. When their skins start to burst you will know that they are ready.

2. You do not need to peel the potatoes. Discard all the water from the pot and use a masher to mash the potatoes. Remove and discard all large pieces of potato skin that get stuck on the masher but leave in the other small bits of skin as it adds to the flavour.

3. Stir in 2 tots of butter or cream and some wasabi paste. The more wasabi you add, the stronger the wasabi flavour in the mash. Add salt and pepper to taste.

PAELLA

The Spanish almost didn't get a mention in this book, but the cult status of paella saved the day!

Catering and kitchen shops sell a type of fireproof steel pan that is perfect for the preparation of this dish, so perfect in fact that this pan is widely referred to as a 'paella pan'. Paella actually means 'pan' and this is where the name of the dish comes from. You will also need this pan for steak flambé (page 38) and *Bratkartoffeln* (see a photo of the pan on page 161) so get yourself one of them. Failing that, any normal cast iron pot also does the job.

WHAT YOU NEED (feeds 8)

Please note that as with most dishes cooked on a braai, paella ingredients are not exact. Take these ingredients as a guideline.

8 chicken pieces (thighs and/or drumsticks)

2 kg shellfish (in the shell – like black mussels and prawns. If you're using just meat without shells, 1 kg is sufficient)

500 g fresh fish fillets (cut into blocks)

250 g spicy cured sausages (sliced or chopped – like chorizo or pepperoni)

2 tots olive oil

1 onion (chopped)

2 peppers (chopped – green, red or yellow)

2 cups rice (uncooked)

2 garlic cloves (crushed or chopped)

1 tsp paprika

1 tsp turmeric

1 tsp chilli powder

4 tomatoes (chopped)

3 cups fish, chicken or vegetable stock (3 cups is 750 ml which is also the size of a wine bottle)

½ cup black olives (pitted)

250 g peas (they come in frozen packets of this size)

1 cup white wine

1 tot parsley (chopped)

salt and pepper

lemon wedges

WHAT TO DO

1. In a large pan on the fire, fry the onions and peppers in the oil for 3 minutes. Your coals should be just hot enough to actually fry the onion. As the steel of the pan is much thinner than a cast-iron pot, it will be a bit more sensitive to heat.

2. Add the rice and mix well. All the rice should be thinly coated with oil. If this is not the case, add a bit more oil. Fry the rice for a few minutes until it turns pale golden in colour. Now add the garlic, paprika, turmeric, chilli powder and chopped tomatoes and stir fry for another 2 minutes.

3. Add the stock and cover the pan with a lid or with tinfoil. The rice should now cook until soft, which will take about 35 minutes in total. Slightly reduce the heat under the pan by scraping away some coals. You are allowed to lift the lid now and again to stir the rice, and to monitor that it is not burning. Should everything seem a bit quiet, scrape a few extra coals back under the pan.

4. After 20 of those 35 minutes, add the seafood, spicy sausage, olives and peas to the pan. Stir it in and cover the pan again. The seafood will cook in these last 15 minutes. Monitor your liquid level and add the wine if the pan becomes dry. If the wine is in and the pan still dry, start adding small amounts of water.

5. On the side, and timing it to be ready with the rest of the dish, braai the chicken pieces in a grid over coals. This will take about 20–25 minutes.

6. When the rice is soft, sample the dish and add salt and pepper to taste.

7. Arrange the chicken pieces on top, garnish with parsley and lemon wedges, and serve immediately.

ANCHOVY AND PECAN NUT PASTA

I discovered this dish during a trip down the Amalfi coast in Italy at a restaurant situated on a rocky beach in a small fishing village. In worse than broken Italian I asked for whatever the chef considers his speciality dish. In front of my eyes a fresh fish was carried from a boat into the restaurant and that same fish was on my table a little while later, with this pasta on the side. As with all my favourite Italian dishes, the ingredients are basic and the preparation simple.

WHAT YOU NEED
(feeds 4 as light main meal,
6 as side dish)

500 g linguini or spaghetti

2 tots olive oil

10 anchovy fillets

4 garlic cloves (finely chopped)

½ cup pecan nuts (in Italy they used walnuts, but pecan nuts are widely available in SA and close enough in taste)

3 tots cream

2 tots chopped parsley

salt and pepper

WHAT TO DO

1. Pound the nuts using a pestle and mortar. Alternatively use a rolling pin or wine bottle to crush them finely on a chopping board.

2. Use a cast iron pot to cook the pasta according to the instructions on the packet. This involves boiling water in a pot, adding salt to that water, and cooking the pasta for roughly 8 minutes in the boiling water (but check the packaging as cooking times differ). If you are at the sea, use fresh seawater that already contains salt for this step. But not seawater with sand.

3. When the pasta is 90% done (just before *al dente*), remove from the pot, drain and set aside. Important: Save some of the water that you boiled the pasta in somewhere, as you will need this later.

4. Add olive oil to the now empty pot and fry the anchovies, garlic and nuts. Stir continuously and use a wooden spoon to press and mash the anchovies until they disintegrate and melt into the oil. This could happen as quickly as in 1 minute so keep a constant eye on the pot and don't try to multitask otherwise it will burn.

5. Add the pasta to the anchovy-and-nut mixture in the pot and stir through. Add the cream and about half a cup of the water that you boiled the pasta in, just enough to create a bit of sauce and to keep the pasta from burning. Let that liquid boil and use a spoon or fork to toss the pasta around a bit. If your pot runs dry, add more water. The amount of water you need to add will depend on the heat and the size and shape of your pot and might differ from one time to the next.

6. As soon as the pasta is heated through again and the sauce thickened to your liking, stir in the parsley. The dish is now ready. Steps 5 and 6 combined should take minutes you can count on one hand.

7. Once it is served up, top the pasta with shavings of pecorino or Parmesan cheese. As the anchovies already added salt to the dish, let each guest add their own salt and pepper to taste.

AND . . .

■ When you get hold of a whole fresh fish, braai that as explained on pages 98 and 100 and serve this pasta on the side.

■ You can also prepare this meal in a normal pot on a stove but it won't be as much fun.

Pork

Pork is like a blank canvas and this means two things: you need to spice it, and it combines well with almost any flavour combination out there. In that way it's similar to chicken. The next character trait pork shares with chicken is that the meat is quite lean, and most of the fat is on the outside. If any particular piece of pork has more fat on it than you like, it's quite easy to trim away. But when doing that, make sure to leave a thin layer of fat on the meat, as it will become crisp and very tasty during the braai. Lastly, as with chicken, pork should not be eaten medium rare; always braai your pork medium (and your chicken done).

Sometimes people mistakenly tell me that they don't like pork on the braai and for them I have three words: pork spare ribs!

HOW TO BRAAI HONEY-GLAZED PORK SPARE RIBS

There are three reasons why pork spare ribs taste so great. First, their relatively high fat content bastes and flavours the meat as it braais; secondly, the high bone-to-meat ratio means that the bones impart further flavour to the meat as they heat up during the braai; thirdly, that sweet and sticky sauce we usually enjoy with them. But marinades and sauces that contain sugar burn easily, so there are two things that can go wrong when you braai spare ribs:

- You remove them from the fire when you think the marinade is starting to burn, but then find the insides still raw.
- You braai them until the inside is done, but by that stage the marinade is burnt.

There is a very easy way to get around these two problems, which is to braai first and marinade later. Don't marinade or baste the ribs, just braai them and remove them from the fire about 5 minutes before they are ready. Generously smother them in the sauce, then return them to the fire and complete the braai. The ribs will be properly cooked inside and your sauce will be nicely glazed without being burnt.

WHAT YOU NEED (feeds 4)

1.5 kg pork spare ribs
½ cup honey (or golden syrup)
½ cup tomato sauce
1 tot apple juice
½ tot soy sauce
½ tot paprika

WHAT TO DO

1. Prepare the sauce: Mix all the ingredients (except for the ribs) together in a bowl. If there is anything else you wish to add to the sauce, do so.

2. Braai the whole spare ribs over medium heat for 30 minutes until almost done.

3. Remove the ribs from the fire and place on a cutting board. Cut into single ribs.

4. Toss the ribs into the sauce bowl and coat them well. Use a spoon or shake the bowl around. Leave for a minute or 3 so that the exposed, meaty parts of the ribs can bond with and absorb the sauce.

5. Braai the now generously basted ribs for between 2 and 10 minutes until all the sauce is warm and glazed. If during the cutting you saw that the ribs were basically done and will start to dry out, just braai them for a minute or 2 until the sauce is glazed, but if you saw they still had a way to go, make it closer to 10 minutes or even longer, also exposing the two recently cut sides of each rib to heat by letting them face the coals.

AND . . .

- I prefer to braai the ribs whole and only cut them before the basting. I feel those exposed parts of meat, where they were cut from each other, then just soak up the marinade a little bit better as they're not sealed. You can also cut the ribs into single riblets or serving portions of three to four before the braai. Time spent on the coals will then be slightly shorter.
- Honey adds a unique flavour to this recipe but you could substitute it with golden syrup.

PORK LOIN CHOPS IN PAPRIKA MARINADE

If you are reading this book from cover to cover (as I suggest you do at least once a year) and provided you've been paying attention, your educated guess that the pork loin chop is the T-bone steak and lamb loin chop of pork would be correct. There is a sirloin and a fillet on either side of the bone and a nice layer of fat running along the side of the sirloin. As with all loin chops, the pork loin chop has a generous layer of fat on the side, which helps with moisture and flavour during the braai. However, sometimes this layer is so thick that people cut it away on their plates. Rather trim the excess fat from pork loin chops before you braai them. Then you'll have a thin, crisp, attractive, tasty layer of fat on the side of your chops when you serve them.

WHAT YOU NEED (feeds 4)

1 kg pork loin or rib chops

1 onion (not too big)

2 cloves garlic

1 tot olive oil

3 tots beer

2 tsp mild to hot mustard

freshly ground pepper

4 chopped sage leaves

2 tsp paprika powder

a few drops chilli sauce

1 lemon

sea salt

WHAT TO DO

1. Fat layer: If it bothers you, cut away the excess fat running along the side of each chop, leaving a thin and even fat layer of acceptable width.

2. Grate or chop the onion and garlic and mix with the oil, beer, mustard, pepper, sage leaves, paprika powder, chilli sauce and juice of the lemon.

3. Coat both sides of each pork chop with this marinade, cover the bowl and let it stand in the fridge for a few hours, preferably overnight.

4. Place the chops on the grid and braai on hot coals, turning often, for about 12 minutes until medium. During this time you can also grind salt and black pepper onto both sides of each chop.

5. Pork loin chops should be served medium. When you cut it on your plate only clear juices should run out, i.e. not pink or red juices. An internal temperature of 71°C in the thickest parts equates to medium – so use your meat thermometer to be sure.

AND . . .

- Even when you do everything right, the pork loin or rib chops might still be dry. That's why I like to serve them with a brown beer sauce (page 136) as I did for the photo opposite. Alternatively, buy some of the really great commercial mustards available in supermarkets and place them on the table when you serve pork.
- You can also braai pork loin chops with the teriyaki-style marinade provided with the pork neck chops on page 126.
- Pork chops go well with a side dish like potato salad (page 180) or Bratkartoffeln (page 160).

PORK NECK CHOPS IN TERIYAKI-STYLE MARINADE

Pork neck chops are a great choice for the braai as they are generally quite tender and have fantastic marbling, with the small bits of fat keeping the meat juicy while imparting flavour.

Pork should be braaied more well-done than beef or lamb. But that means there is an increased risk that the meat will be dry by the time it is ready to eat. So, marinating pork is a good idea as it has a brining effect, which increases your margin of error to braai pork medium, yet still keep it juicy.

WHAT YOU NEED (feeds 4)

1 kg pork neck chops

2 tots soy sauce

2 tots sherry (the old brown type will do)

2 tots honey

2 garlic cloves (finely chopped or crushed)

ginger (chopped and equal in quantity to garlic)

salt and pepper (to taste when serving)

WHAT TO DO

1. Combine all the marinade ingredients and then mix in with the chops, ensuring all sides are coated with marinade. Cover the bowl and leave to marinate for a few hours or overnight in the fridge. If you feel that some chops aren't in touch with enough of the marinade then stir, toss or reverse the order of the chops a few times during this time.

2. Braai over hot coals for about 10-15 minutes until medium. Remember that there is sugar in your marinade and that you want to braai the chops medium all the way through. Guard against burning the chops – turn more often than when you braai steak, and braai on milder heat.

3. During the braai you can baste the chops with any leftover marinade but do not baste during the last 5 minutes of the braai as you might then contaminate your chops with raw meat juices. Alternatively, boil the marinade for a few minutes and serve as a sauce over the chops.

AND . . .

For the real teriyaki sauce recipe, that goes very well as a marinade or sauce with pretty much any meat, turn to page 136.

Sauces

- -

All the sauces in this chapter are easy and straightforward to prepare and you should be able to make them with one eye while keeping your other eye on the fire.

Also look out for sauces that are described in other chapters, particularly:

Tomato-chilli relish on page 94

Tzatziki on page 62

Garlic, lemon and butter sauce on page 106.

MADAGASCAN GREEN PEPPERCORN SAUCE

The trick to making this peppercorn sauce is locating the green peppercorns in the supermarket. They are sold in small glass jars and are usually hidden away on a shelf somewhere in the vicinity of the olives.

WHAT YOU NEED (feeds 4)

3 tots green peppercorns (drained)

1 tot butter

1 tot brandy

1 cup fresh cream
(or ½ cream ½ cream cheese)

1 tot lemon juice

1 tot Dijon mustard

WHAT TO DO

1. Drain the peppercorns. Keep 2 tots whole and crush 1 tot of the peppercorns in a pestle and mortar. Then sauté the lot in the butter for 2 minutes. Sauté means to fry in a pan with butter or oil.

2. Add the brandy. If you do not want alcohol in the sauce, flambé it now. To flambé means to set the ingredients of the pan alight so that the alcohol burns off.

3. Add all the other ingredients, heat, and stir continuously until the sauce starts to boil. It's now ready. Reheat it before serving.

MONKEYGLAND SAUCE

This is a great sauce for burgers or steaks. Personally I think it's a bit overpowering for that 28-day dry-aged T-bone, but perfect for adding flavour to normal supermarket steaks. It also goes well with home-braaied burgers (page 32). As South Africa is the world leader when it comes to the quality of our chutney and tomato sauce, the two anchor ingredients of the sauce, it should come as no surprise that this sauce is a South African invention.

WHAT YOU NEED (feeds 6-8)

1 large onion (finely chopped)

1 tot butter or oil

2 cloves garlic (finely chopped)

1 cup tomato sauce

1 cup chutney

½ cup Worcestershire sauce

1 tot brown sugar

1 tot vinegar

chilli flakes, fresh chilli or chilli sauce (to taste)

water (have some on standby in case your pot runs dry)

WHAT TO DO

1. In a pot on the fire or stove, fry the onion in the butter or oil for 4 minutes until golden.

2. Add all the other ingredients except for the chilli and water and simmer for 15 minutes, stirring fairly often to make sure it doesn't burn. If the pot runs dry and the sauce is too thick for your liking or starts to burn, add a little bit of water.

3. Taste the sauce while it's cooking and if you want to add more bite to it, add a bit of chilli powder, chilli flakes, fresh chilli or a chilli sauce.

4. After 15 minutes of simmering the sauce is ready to serve. You can now keep it warm until the meat is ready, or start pouring it generously over hamburgers and steaks straight away.

MUSHROOM SAUCE

There are many mushroom sauce recipes. All the good ones have the same basics, which is to fry some mushrooms, add cream and cheese, and then let it simmer.

This one is from my sister Ina Mari, and is my favourite. When the family gets together for Christmas, among other things we usually braai a whole sirloin and then this sauce goes onto the table.

WHAT YOU NEED
(feeds 4–6)

500 g mushrooms (finely chopped)
1 tot olive oil
1 cup cream
1 tsp braai spice powder (I humbly suggest the Jan Braai signature spice, available at all leading supermarkets)
salt and pepper
1 egg
½ cup cream cheese

WHAT TO DO

1. Fry the chopped mushrooms in the oil until soft.

2. Add the cream, salt, pepper and braai spice and bring to the boil.

3. Beat the egg and then add about half a cup of the warm cream-and-mushroom mix to the egg, stirring continuously.

4. Now add this egg mix back to the rest of the mushroom cream in the pot.

5. Stir in the cream cheese until everything is combined, and heat until the mixture simmers.

AND . . .

■ You can replace the braai spice with any other spice you fancy, but our original family recipe uses braai spice.
■ If you're feeling lazy, leave out the egg.
■ The ½ cup cream cheese can be replaced with ½ cup of any normal cheese like Cheddar or Gouda – just grate it before stirring it in.
■ There's nothing stopping you from adding a glass of white wine to this sauce. It is a well-known fact that white wine complements mushrooms, cream and cheese.

MUSTARD SAUCE

This is how to make mustard sauce but the exact taste will depend on your choice of mustard. Experiment by using a combination of different mustards, for example half Dijon, half wholegrain, and see what you like best.

WHAT YOU NEED
a little butter
2 units mustard (your favourite or even a combination of different ones)
2 units cream
1 unit white wine
salt and pepper (to taste)

WHAT TO DO

1. In a pan melt some butter and then add equal amounts of mustard and cream and half that amount of white wine.

2. Mix very well until you have a smooth sauce that is uniform in colour.

3. Add salt and pepper to taste.

4. Heat the sauce until it starts to boil and then remove it from the heat. It is now ready to serve with steak, pork, chicken or hamburgers.

AND . . .

If the mustard is very strong and the sauce is too hot, add more cream. You can really add anything you want to this basic mustard sauce. My favourite steakhouse in Cape Town, for example, serves a delicious mustard and caper sauce.

PERI-PERI SAUCE

In this book I use the peri-peri sauce with three specific recipes but in real braai life you will use it more often. It goes particularly well with braaied steak, chicken, fish and prawns.

Due to the combination of ingredients it will easily last for weeks in your fridge and the flavour gets even better after standing for a few days. I suggest you make it in large quantities.

WHAT YOU NEED

(feeds 10, but if your sauce is very hot it might feed more)

8 cloves garlic (finely chopped)

½ cup oil

½ cup grape vinegar (red or white)

½ cup lemon juice

½ cup water

1 tot paprika powder

1 tot chilli powder

1 tot salt

a few small hot chillies
(Piri-Piri/African Bird's Eye – chopped)

WHAT TO DO

1. Finely chop the garlic and throw this into a glass bottle or jar with the oil, vinegar, lemon juice, water, paprika powder, chilli powder and salt. Shake well until the ingredients are mixed and all the salt dissolved.

2. Now taste the sauce and if you want it hotter, add a few finely chopped chillies to the sauce and shake. You can add as many chillies as you wish but remember that you can never expect your guests to eat a sauce that is too hot for them. If, like me, you like quite a lot of burn then it might be wise to mix two batches, one with fewer chillies.

3. Do not touch your eyes or any other sensitive parts of your body while you are making this sauce as the traces of chilli juice left on your hands will burn those sensitive parts. Go and wash your hands to get the chilli juices off them, and then still be careful.

4. The sauce can be used immediately but will improve with age and last in your fridge for weeks.

AND . . .

The use of peri-peri chillies and sauces filtered into South Africa from our Portuguese-speaking neighbouring countries Mozambique and Angola. The peri-peri (also called African Bird's Eye or Piri-Piri) chilli is a member of the *Capsicum* family of chillies. Compared to the average chilli it's quite small and very hot. If you can't get hold of it, use any small and potent chilli. But best is to get yourself a plant and cultivate them at home; they grow quite easily in most parts of South Africa. In the photo on the opposite page you can see what they look like.

INGREDIENT MEASUREMENTS FOR ONCE-OFF USE

Sometimes you don't need a whole jar of peri-peri so then use these quantities: 1 tot oil, 1 tot vinegar, 1 tot lemon juice, 1 tot water, 1 tsp paprika, 1 tsp chilli powder, 1 tsp salt, 2 cloves chopped garlic, 1 or more small hot chillies.

TERIYAKI SAUCE

This classic sauce from Japan can be made as a marinade, basting or sauce to accompany fish, steak, pork or chicken. I wouldn't eat it with lamb, but if you really want to, go ahead.

WHAT YOU NEED
(feeds 4)

½ cup dark soy sauce

½ cup dry sherry

½ cup sweet sherry

1 tot mix of chopped garlic and ginger

1 tot sugar

WHAT TO DO FOR MARINADE OR BASTING

1. Mix all the ingredients together until the sugar is dissolved and that's it!

WHAT TO DO FOR SAUCE

1. Mix all the ingredients together in a pan and bring to the boil.

2. Simmer for 15 minutes until it starts to thicken. You can serve it hot or cold.

BROWN BEER SAUCE

This sauce goes down very well; German beer gardens serve it with pork and in Ireland it is served with chicken. It has a lot of flavour and is your perfect solution to that somewhat dry piece of meat.

There are two steps that might look tricky - reducing and straining - but both are really simple. To reduce something you just boil it until half of the liquid evaporates. It means that the liquid that is left has double the taste. Then there is straining the sauce, which means you have to filter out the solids and keep the liquid.

To see what it looks like, go to page 125 where there is a photo of this brown beer sauce served with pork loin chops.

WHAT YOU NEED
(feeds 2–4)

1 onion (sliced or chopped)

½ cup butter

2 tots fresh herbs (parsley, sage, rosemary, thyme, rocket, basil, marjoram, oregano – whatever you have on hand)

1 tin or bottle of dark beer

1 tot honey

1 tsp lemon juice

salt and pepper (to taste)

WHAT TO DO

1. In a pan, fry the onion and herbs in the butter until the onion is golden brown.

2. Add the beer and simmer until the liquid has reduced by half. This takes a while.

3. Strain the sauce (a sieve works best). Keep the liquid, discard the solids. If you haven't got a sieve or other suitable filter to do this job, or feel that this step is too complicated, simply take a spoon or fork and remove all the big pieces of onion and herbs floating around in the sauce.

4. Add the honey and lemon juice, heat and stir. Adjust with salt and pepper to taste and the sauce is ready.

CHIMICHURRI SAUCE

Argentina is the one other nation that almost plays in our league when it comes to making fires and cooking meat on those fires, and the one ever-present item at these meals is a sauce known as chimichurri. The sauce is used as a marinade, or as a basting or dipping sauce and there is no standard recipe, with every household mixing up their own batch. It's enjoyed with anything from steak to chicken and fish.

WHAT YOU NEED (feeds 4–6)

1 onion (very finely chopped or even grated)

3 tots chopped parsley

1 tot oregano (fresh and chopped, or dried)

1 tot chopped garlic

½ tot salt

½ tot paprika

1 tsp chilli (fresh and chopped, or powder – more or less to taste)

½ cup olive oil

2 tots red wine vinegar

black pepper

WHAT TO DO

1. Wash the fresh herbs well so that there's no sand in your sauce.

2. Combine all the ingredients, except for the oil, vinegar and black pepper, using a pestle and mortar. If you don't have a pestle and mortar then put them in a bowl, mix them very well and make a note to go and buy a pestle and mortar.

3. Pour the oil and vinegar into a jar or bowl, add the other well-mixed ingredients and stir thoroughly. Now cover the sauce and let it stand for at least an hour before you use it; a day or two is even better. This gives the flavours time to 'develop'.

4. Add black pepper and possibly more salt to taste.

AND . . .

Almost all ingredients of chimichurri sauce are optional so if there is something you don't have or don't like, leave it out. In the same way, if there is something you want to add, do so. This is your opportunity to create a personalised sauce, tailor-made for your taste buds.

SERVING SUGGESTION: RUMP STEAK WITH CHIMICHURRI SAUCE

1. Braai one big rump steak medium rare. Do it over very hot coals and turn it once. It will take about 7 minutes in total.

2. Take the steak off the fire, put it on a cutting board and plaster it with a layer of chimichurri sauce. The recipe above gives you enough sauce for more than one steak.

3. Let the meat rest for 3 minutes and then slice the steak into strips. Try to slice at a 45-degree angle, which allows you to cut across the grain of the meat an additional time.

4. Serve to everybody around the fire as a snack. The rest of the sauce can be used as a dipping sauce or marinade for steak, chicken or fish.

Potjies
Cast-iron pots

TYPES OF *POTJIES*

THREE-LEGGED POT

The most common of all cast-iron pots is the three-legged *potjie*. As it comes with legs attached to the body it is the most stable when standing in a fireplace, as the other types still need to be balanced on a separate stand. In a cruel twist of fate, however, the three-legged *potjie* is the most unstable and difficult to transport. (If you ever need to transport one, take the lid off and place it upside down in the boot of your car.)

BAKE POT

The second type of pot is the bake pot and is completely flat-bottomed. It has no legs, is not round when viewed from the side and is shallow compared to the other two types. This is the only pot that you can bake bread in and it is better suited to other baked dishes like lasagne. Thanks to its more open-topped shape, it's also the best one to use if you like to take photos of your food. Due to its flat bottom, this pot can also double up as a pan to cook eggs in while camping. (But then again, you can simply make scrambled eggs in your three-legged one.) Of all the shapes, this one is the easiest to transport but you will need a separate tripod to rest it on in the fireplace.

PLATPOTJIE

The *platpotjie* is a hybrid between the three-legged and the bake pot. It's round when viewed from the side (all pots are round when viewed from the top) and deep, like the three-legged one, but does not have legs. It has a small flat area at the bottom. The disadvantage is that you need a separate tripod to balance the pot on but the advantage is that you can use it on an electric or gas stove in those situations where you need to do so, plus it travels more easily. If your pot is going to hang from a hook in your built-in braai, then obviously the absence of legs makes no difference. But if your house has a built-in braai, this discussion about pots is not really for you, as you should by right own at least one of each shape, but preferably more, in various sizes.

HOW TO PREPARE A NEWLY PURCHASED *POTJIE* FOR USE

A *potjie* is made from cast iron. As such, there are some unsavoury elements inside your new pot upon purchase. Cooking food in a brand-new pot is a very bad idea as the food will not only look funny (it will have an unnatural dark colour even though you haven't burnt it) but it will also taste like iron. Preparing your new pot is a very important yet simple procedure. The first step is to wash and scrub it properly using warm water, dishwashing liquid and steel wool. Dry it and then completely coat the inside with cooking oil (cheap sunflower will do the trick). Heat the pot until the oil begins to smoke and then wipe it clean with a paper towel. Repeat this oil, heat and wiping drill until the paper towel comes out clean. Now wash the pot and test whether it's ready by cooking maize meal porridge in it (page 144 or page 146). If the porridge comes out white and tastes fine, your pot is ready for general use, and you have porridge.

MAINTENANCE

Wash your *potjie* using warm water, dishwashing liquid and steel wool. Dry it well afterwards and store it with lots of crumpled old newspapers stuffed inside it. The paper will absorb moisture and keep it from rusting too badly. If it does show a bit of rust, just wash and scrub it off. Rinse the pot before using it and if you have not used it for a while, wash it. Some people coat their pots with cooking oil during storage to guard against rust but that oil becomes a bit sticky and disgusting after a while so I steer away from it. If you go that route, wash the pot properly before every use.

You will find three classic *potjie* recipes elsewhere in this book under the chapters of their respective types of meat:
- For the Oxtail *potjie*, go to page 42.
- For the Lamb shank (or lamb neck) *potjie*, go to page 60.
- For the Chicken curry *potjie*, go to page 86.

PUTU PAP IN A *POTJIE* (ALSO KNOWN AS *KRUMMELPAP*)

There are but three principles to successfully making *putu pap*. They are:
1. managing the water:maize meal ratio,
2. building an iceberg, and
3. using a two-tined fork.

WHAT YOU NEED (feeds 5-6)

3 cups maize meal

2 cups water

1 tsp salt

WHAT TO DO

1. Bring the water to the boil and add the salt.

2. Remove the pot from the flames.

3. Pour all the maize meal into the water aiming for the centre of the pot. You should now have an 'iceberg' of maize meal in the pot, with the lower part under water and the top part sticking out of the water in the centre.

4. Put the lid on and place a few coals under the pot. You want a slight bubble from the water every now and again, but essentially the rest of the water now needs to steam into the maize meal.

5. You can check once or twice that there is enough heat and that steam is in fact being generated, but don't check too often as steam will escape every time you lift the lid, and that steam is supposed to go into the maize meal, not into the clear blue sky.

6. After 20 minutes remove the lid and use the two-tined fork to break the iceberg. Vigorously stir all the porridge and any leftover water drifting around in the pot until the contents look like *putu pap*.

7. If you think it all looks a bit dry, add some water (cold or hot) and stir it in with the two-tined fork.

8. Replace the lid and let it continue to steam on gentle heat for another 20 minutes.

AND . . .

As you can see, this recipe is very easy. For more *putu pap*, increase your ingredients but stick to the same ratio. It's quite common for the maize meal to form a crust at the bottom of the pot. Do not worry about this. Simply treat the top of this crust as the new 'bottom' of your pot. After the whole process is finished and all the porridge has been eaten, this crust can be removed quite easily. You can even heat the pot just before removing the crust and then eat the crust with a bit of butter.

STYWE PAP IN A POTJIE

WHAT YOU NEED (feeds 3–4)

3 cups water

2 cups maize meal

1 tsp salt

WHAT TO DO

1. Pour 2 of the 3 cups of water and the teaspoon of salt into a pot and get the water boiling: If you're cooking with a fire, place the pot on the flames; if you're making it on a stove, set the temperature to whatever the highest setting is.

2. In a separate bowl, mix the 2 cups of maize meal with the remaining cup of water. The water you use should be normal room temperature water from a tap or bottle. My father taught this step to me – it is important and should be done properly. If you throw all the maize meal straight into the boiling water your chances of lumps forming in the porridge are greatly increased.

3. As soon as the water in the pot boils, stir this maize meal-and-water mixture into the boiling water using a wooden spoon. Mixing it in properly should take you between 1 and 2 minutes.

4. Put the lid on the pot and let it simmer for 25 minutes on low heat. On a fire this means removing the pot from the flames and placing it on a few coals.

5. You may check on the *pap* once or twice during this time to make sure it's simmering (not boiling – too hot; or standing still – too cold) but don't lift the lid to often as too much water will then escape in the form of steam. After 25 minutes the *pap* will be ready.

AND . . .

■ Don't worry if there is a little crust burnt onto the inside bottom of the pot. This sometimes happens. That crust easily lifts out of the pot and is considered a delicacy in my family, enjoyed with a bit of butter.

■ *Slap pap* (runny maize meal porridge) is made in exactly the same way as above, except you use 2½ or even 3 cups of water in step 1 and still use 1 cup of water in step 2. Personally I prefer *stywe pap* with braaied meat as it can be served on a plate and eaten with a knife and fork, or with your hands.

■ There are many different brands of maize meal on the market and they are all essentially the same thing: dried maize kernels milled to various degrees of fineness. I prefer those that are milled a little bit coarser but this is a personal preference. Use whichever brand you prefer, they are basically all the same. To summarise, the best one is the cheapest one.

BRAAI LASAGNE *POTJIE*

After every braai, if there is any leftover meat, debone and skin the meat. Then chop it up finely and add it to the container in your freezer that is specially placed there for this purpose. As soon as you have enough meat in that container, make the braai lasagne *potjie*.

WHAT YOU NEED (feeds 4–6)
12 lasagne sheets
butter

For the bolognese sauce:
500 g finely chopped leftover braaied meat (any mixture of steak, chops, pork, chicken, boerewors)
1 onion (finely chopped)
1 clove garlic (finely chopped)
1 cup mix of grated carrots and finely chopped celery
1 tot butter
½ cup dry red wine
2 tins chopped tomatoes
1 tot tomato paste
1 tot oregano
1 bay leaf
1 tsp salt
1 tsp pepper

For the béchamel (white) sauce:
3 tots butter
3 tots flour
2 cups stock (vegetable, beef, chicken, etc., whatever you have on hand. Alternatively 1 cup stock and 1 cup milk)
½ cup cream
½ cup grated Parmesan cheese (or aged cheddar, but then use more)
½ tsp nutmeg
salt and pepper

WHAT TO DO

1. Make the bolognese sauce: In the pot that you will bake the lasagne in, mix the onion, garlic, carrot and celery and fry gently in the butter until soft. Some light flames should give you the correct heat. If it boils too rapidly, remove the pot from the flames and heat it with a few coals. Add the meat, wine, tomatoes, tomato paste, oregano, bay leaf, salt and pepper. Stir very well then simmer for 10–15 minutes, stirring now and then. Keep the cooked sauce in another container until you need it for Step 3.

2. Make the béchamel sauce: In a separate pot, melt the butter and use a wooden spoon to mix the flour completely into the melted butter. Now add the stock bit by bit while you continuously stir the mixture. When all the stock has been added, let the sauce simmer for a few minutes. Remove from the heat and stir in the cream, Parmesan and nutmeg. Add salt and pepper to taste.

3. Make the lasagne: Fill the cast-iron pot with layers of bolognese sauce, pasta sheets and béchamel sauce. A flat-bottomed pot will result in a neater lasagne but any round-bottomed pot is also fine.

4. Put the lid on the pot and bake the lasagne for about 50 minutes by placing the pot on a stand over coals and also putting a few coals on the lid of the pot. When all the pasta sheets are completely soft, the lasagne is ready.

PUTTANESCA PASTA IN A *POTJIE*

Some people could have long debates on whether a recipe like this belongs in a braai book. The fact of the matter is that, to my mind, something delicious prepared in a cast-iron pot over an open fire is much closer to the essence of braaing than grilling a steak on a gas braai.

Puttanesca pasta is one of the true Italian classics, and something you really should master. The dish can be made entirely from non-perishable ingredients making it a great meal to prepare when out on a camping trip or safari. This can be served as a light lunch or dinner on its own, but puttanesca pasta also works very well as the second course of your five-course braai.

WHAT YOU NEED

(feeds 4 as main and 6–8 as side)

500 g spaghetti
1 tot salt
3 tots olive oil
1 big onion (chopped)
8 anchovy fillets
5 cloves of garlic (chopped)
1 red chilli (seeded and chopped)
1 tot capers, drained
½–1 cup black olives (drained and pitted)
2 tins peeled and chopped tomatoes
2 tots tomato paste
1 tot fresh parsley (chopped)
salt and pepper
basil leaves (for garnish)

WHAT TO DO

1. Cook the pasta by the placing the pot on the fire and bringing 4 litres of water to the boil. Add 1 tot of salt to this (yes, this is really necessary but don't worry, most of this salt will be thrown away with the water). Only add the pasta when the water is boiling properly. Spaghetti takes about 8 minutes to cook *al dente*, but you will have to check the packaging of the brand you are using, and monitor its progress in the pot. You want to remove the pasta and drain it in a colander when it is 95% done.

2. Add the olive oil and chopped onion to the empty pot and return it to fire. Lightly fry the onion for about 4 minutes.

3. Add the anchovies, garlic and chilli and fry for another 2 minutes, breaking up the anchovies with your wooden spoon until they dissolve into the oil. (If you don't have a wooden spoon, buy one.)

4. Add the capers, olives, tomatoes and tomato paste. Stir well and simmer this sauce for about 10 minutes, stirring occasionally.

5. Add ground pepper and salt to taste. Go easy on the salt as the anchovies and capers already add saltiness to the pot.

6. Add the spaghetti and parsley and toss together well for a minute or 2 until everything is properly mixed and the pasta is heated again.

7. Dish up straight from the pot and garnish each serving on its plate with a basil leaf.

AND . . .

- You can obviously use other pasta as well but I like spaghetti.
- You can also use two different pots but I prefer this method as it means there is less to clean afterwards.
- The pasta will cook a bit more when it's added to the sauce again and, as cast iron retains its heat for a while, it will also continue to cook even after the pot is removed from the fire before you serve up. That is why you want to remove the pasta from the water before it is completely cooked.
- Keep some of the water you used to boil the pasta in. If the dish gets too dry when you add the pasta again at the end (if your fire is very hot and your pot lost too much moisture) then add some of this liquid instead of plain water.

Vegetables

As you well know, anything tastes better when it's braaied and vegetables are no exception. The reason why braaied vegetables taste so good is that the heat from the fire caramelises the natural plant sugars in the vegetables making them taste sweeter.

These days the price of meat, it seems, only varies between expensive and very expensive. Vegetables are different though. They still tend to go in and out of season and the ones that are in season not only taste the best, they are also priced most favourably. My point is that the best vegetable to braai is the one that is in season at that particular time.

Don't forget there's a *soetpatat* recipe on page 104 in the Seafood chapter too.

COAL-BAKED POTATO

I often attend braais where these potatoes are considered as natural a side dish as boerewors and *braaibroodjies*. On other occasions, people have never heard of preparing them in this way. All I know is that both potatoes and tinfoil last quite a while outside a fridge which makes this a perfect side dish at many of the near and far-flung places where people gather around braai fires.

WHAT YOU NEED (per person)

medium to large potato

sour cream (or cream cheese, cottage cheese or crème fraîche)

chives (finely chopped – they might be growing in your herb garden but buy a bunch or pack if they are not, and use parsley if you can't get hold of chives)

salt and pepper

tinfoil

WHAT TO DO

1. Wash the potatoes in or under cold water and then wrap each potato tightly in tinfoil. No need to carefully dry them, just wrap them up. Take them to the fire immediately.

2. Potatoes take longer than the average piece of braai meat to get done in this fashion and you want to give them good, but not furious, heat. I usually place them at the edge of my fire and then position the odd coal around and on top of them. When the fire has burnt out and the coals are spread open, just put them all along the border of your circle of coals. Assuming your fire takes about 40 minutes to burn out and your meat braais for 10–15 minutes, the potatoes will be ready with the meat. To test whether they are done, press on each one with your tongs and if they are soft and yielding you know that they are ready; alternatively, pierce the potato with a knife through the foil and check whether the knife goes in easily. Remember that not all of them will take exactly the same time, as their positioning in the coals will make a difference.

3. Using tongs, remove the potatoes from the fire and shake off all the ash. If your guests are from Europe, use a cloth to wipe the last traces of ash off the foil.

4. Cut a cross into the top of each potato through the tinfoil using a chef's or bread knife.

5. Use your thumbs and forefingers to press each potato from four sides so that the top opens like a flower.

6. Spoon some sour cream, cream cheese or crème fraîche into each potato and top with chives.

AND . . .

- This recipe works equally well with sweet potato.
- You can use salted butter instead of cream or cheese but it doesn't look as impressive.

ONIONS IN THE COALS

Onions can be successfully baked in the coals of your fire whether they are wrapped in foil or not. As with potatoes, they should be placed at the edge of your coals. The first option is to peel and wrap them in foil. If you go this route, add a little butter, garlic butter, olive oil, balsamic vinegar or wine to each one before you wrap them up. Alternatively you can braai them in the coals unpeeled, as is. In both cases they will take about 20–30 minutes to get done. Remove from the coals with braai tongs, shake off the ash and optionally wipe them with a cloth before serving them. If you braaied them without foil, the outside layer (or three) will obviously not be edible and needs to be discarded.

MEALIES (CORN)

Considering how great they taste, I only started eating braaied mealies quite late in my life. It was a few years ago in the middle of the old Transkei during a fairly tough day, which involved my (then) Land Rover breaking down in the middle of nowhere. A lady next to the road was selling braaied mealies for R1 each, which was very cheap even then. I sat down at the side of the road under a tree with the mealie and a quart of beer from a local shebeen and for a moment, life seemed OK. I've not stopped eating braaied mealies since then.

WHAT YOU NEED (per person)
mealie
butter
salt

WHAT TO DO

1. When buying mealies in a supermarket or greengrocer, try and get some that still have part of the husk on them (or are still completely in the husk). Supermarkets often sell mealies that are packaged with one side exposed and the other side covered by husk. Those are the ones you want.

2. Pack the mealies side by side on the hinged braai grid, green leaves facing down and exposed yellow kernel side facing up, and close the grid.

3. Braai the mealies on hot coals for about 10–15 minutes until done. During this time you want the green husk side to face the coals about 70% of the time and the exposed yellow kernels the rest of the time. Don't worry about the leaves getting burnt as this is supposed to happen. If the sides don't get enough heat, slightly turn the mealies at some stage.

4. When the exposed yellow kernels are nicely browned and caramelised and the husk side is completely burnt, the mealies are ready. Remove them from the fire and place in the one half of a braai bowl – don't put a lid on them because the steam they generate will ruin the crispiness they got on the braai.

5. Take the mealies one by one and remove, pull and scrape off all the remaining husks. The kernels that were under the husks will be wonderfully soft and sweet and the kernels that were exposed to direct heat will have a rich and robust braaied mealie flavour.

6. Smear each mealie with a bit of butter (I find that a dessertspoon works better than a knife for this) and grind salt over them.

AND . . .

When you manage to get hold of mealies that are still completely in the husk, braai them directly on the coals exactly as they come turning them now and then. They will steam, cook and braai perfectly just like that. As soon as a kernel starts to show through the husk, i.e. when the leaves start to burn away in some part, that mealie is ready to be enjoyed.

BUTTERNUT WITH A FILLING

This dish is the fancy cousin of the potato baked in foil. It is incredibly simple to prepare yet never fails to impress people who are not used to it.

WHAT YOU NEED
(each butternut feeds 2)

butternuts

filling of your choice (see below)

a roll of tinfoil

Filling (choose one)

creamed spinach and mushroom (made by lightly frying mushroom and chopped spinach and mixing that with cream cheese)

garlic and herb butter (made by mixing garlic, herbs and butter)

onion, pepper and feta (fry onion and sweet pepper then mix with crumbled feta)

sweetcorn (made by opening a tin of sweetcorn or creamed sweetcorn)

WHAT TO DO

1. Do not peel the butternuts!

2. Slice each butternut in half using a big sharp knife. Use a spoon to scrape out the pips and strings from the cavity.

3. Load the cavities with the filling of your choice.

4. Tightly wrap each butternut in tinfoil and pack them on coals at the edge of the heat zone of your fire. Position a few coals around and on top of each butternut. To cook them evenly, rotate the butternuts occasionally or move and adjust the coals.

5. They are done when their flesh yields under the foil when you press them with braai tongs. This should take about 40 minutes. Alternatively, insert a knife into them through the foil and if the knife goes in easily they are ready. Each guest gets half a butternut and can open the foil themselves to see and smell the aroma of the steam as it escapes.

6. Half a butternut plus filling is quite a significant serving of vegetable but it really gets a bit messy to subdivide it further. Just make sure you serve at least two types of meat to keep the universe in balance.

AND . . .

Try and get nice small butternuts so that half a butternut can be served to each person. Bigger butternuts also work, but they will take closer to an hour to cook and you might have to slice them up further before serving which does not look as attractive on a plate.

BRATKARTOFFELN – THE GERMAN CLASSIC

Bratkartoffeln is to Germans what French fries are to Americans. It's the default side dish to pork, chicken, steak and fish (Germans don't really eat lamb very often).

WHAT YOU NEED

(side dish for 6)

1 kg potatoes

2 tots butter

1 tot oil (vegetable or olive)

2 onions (finely chopped)

6 slices rindless bacon (cut into small pieces)

2 tots chopped parsley

salt and black pepper

WHAT TO DO

1. Do not peel the potatoes yet. Boil them in their skins until just before they are done, i.e. tender but still firm. This will take about 20 minutes and can be done hours in advance or even the previous day. Remove from the water and let them cool down slightly for 10 minutes.

2. Peel the potatoes. No need for a potato peeler, just pull the skins off with the aid of a knife.

3. Now let the potatoes cool down completely. You can even store them in a fridge during this time.

4. Cut the boiled, peeled potatoes into slices 5 mm (½ cm) thick. Alternatively, cut into small cubes.

5. Use a large steel pan (the same one you need to make the flambéed steaks on page 38 and paella on page 116), add half of the oil and butter to it and fry the potato pieces for a few minutes on both sides until they start turning golden brown. You need a large pan so as to expose all the potatoes to the bottom of the pan and thus get them 'frying' instead of 'steaming'. If your pan is not big enough, split all the ingredients in half and perform steps 5, 6 and 7 twice.

6. Add the onions, bacon and rest of the oil and butter to the pan and continue to fry the whole lot until the onions are golden and translucent, the bacon is done and the potatoes are nicely browned and crispy. You want to be careful when turning the potatoes, as the idea is to create this dish without breaking or mashing too many of them. A large spatula works best.

7. Finally add the parsley and season generously with salt and black pepper to taste.

VEGETABLES, SKEWERED OR IN A BRAAI PAN

Braai-wise there are two types of vegetables: those that can be eaten raw and those that need to be cooked. The easiest way and only real trick to braaing vegetables successfully is to separate the two types.

EXAMPLES OF VEGETABLES THAT NEED TO BE COOKED THROUGH:

Potato, sweet potato, butternut, pumpkin, bigger chunks of carrot, whole baby onions, aubergines.

EXAMPLES OF VEGETABLES THAT CAN BE EATEN RAW OR CRUNCHY:

Peppers (red, yellow and green), thin slices of carrot, mushrooms, green beans, baby marrow, onion pieces, green asparagus, baby corn – in short, anything that you find on those health platters at cocktail parties.

WHAT TO DO

1. Vegetables should be braaied on medium to slightly hot coals. The vegetables that need to be cooked through usually take a significantly longer time to braai than the ones that can be eaten raw or chunky. If you are braaing vegetables on skewers then make separate skewers from the two types or pre-boil the vegetables that need to be cooked through before skewering them with their less demanding counterparts. If you are using a braai pan, start off the hard vegetables well in advance before adding the easier ones.

2. The skewers of vegetables that all need to be cooked must be braaied until the last vegetables are soft all the way through. In the case of skewers with vegetables that can be eaten raw or crunchy, simply braai them until the first item on the skewer is soft; you'll then have a nice mix of sweet and caramelised vegetables with a bit of crunch.

3. The preparation of all these vegetables is the same. After they are washed, peeled and chopped, place them in a bowl and drizzle olive oil over them. Add some salt and finely chopped herbs of your choice. Toss the vegetables around until all are thinly coated with oil. They are now ready to be skewered and braaied or braaied in the pan.

MUSHROOM BURGERS

This is a revolutionary burger. It's the vegetarian meal that meat-eaters love. I like to make them using those normal supermarket hamburger rolls with no substance, as it keeps the focus on the mushroom.

WHAT YOU NEED (feeds 6)

6 giant mushrooms

6 soft hamburger rolls

plain cream cheese

feta cheese (I like the kind with bits of black pepper but any type will do)

garlic butter

WHAT TO DO

1. Slice the rolls and spread cream cheese onto the bottom half of each roll.

2. Braai the mushrooms on medium to hot coals until nicely browned and fairly soft, for a total of about 6–8 minutes. Braai them for 3 minutes with the bottom (black) side facing downwards. Then flip them over, scoop a bit of garlic butter into each and then braai with the top (white) side facing downwards until they are soft. They turn quite easily and if you are gentle they will not break apart so either an open or hinged grid is fine.

3. Put one mushroom on each prepared roll and crumble feta cheese over that.

4. The burgers can be eaten immediately and juices from the mushrooms will seep into the roll as you eat.

WHAT TO DO FOR GARLIC BUTTER

Very simply you mix chopped garlic and butter. If you have parsley on hand you chop that and mix it in as well. For 6 mushrooms you'll need 1–2 tots of butter, 1–2 cloves of garlic and ½ tot of parsley.

AUBERGINE

The aubergine goes by many names and I usually call it a brinjal; but considering that the spell checker of the word-processing program that I used to type this book did not think that brinjal was a word, I went with aubergine for the heading. Another name often used for this vegetable is eggplant. The brinjal has as many uses on the braai as it has names. Brinjal skins can be eaten and you don't need to peel them for any of the recipes below.

MAKE CHIPS

1. Thinly slice each brinjal lengthwise and lie the slices on a clean surface. Now salt each slice with a bit of coarse sea salt. The salt will draw out some water and assist you in the mission of making crisp chips.

2. When the fire is burnt out and the coals are ready, shake or scrape off all the salt and dry each slice with paper towel. Braai each slice for a minute or two on both sides on hot coals. Each slice takes quite a bit of braai-grid space so you might need more than one grid or you'll have to do the braai in batches. If you want to make the effort, paint the slices with olive oil during the braai.

3. Serve the brinjal chips to guests around the braai.

AS A SIDE DISH

Slice each brinjal in thicker slices of about 1 cm each and grind salt onto them. Leave until the coals are ready, then shake or scrape off the salt and pat dry with paper towel. Braai over medium heat until browned and soft. Paint with olive oil during the braai. Serve as a side dish.

MAKE A SALAD

1. Braai thicker slices of brinjal as described above and remove from the fire when ready. Brinjal slices physically change colour as they cook – similar to onions or chicken breasts. When you braai them you will see what I mean. When all the white is gone, they are ready.

2. Cut each slice into squares of about 2 cm × 2 cm.

3. Chop 1 pepper (red, yellow or green), 1 onion and 2 cloves of garlic, and fry the lot in a bit of olive oil for a minute or 3.

4. Chop 4 big tomatoes (or a host of cherry tomatoes) and 2 feta cheese wheels.

5. Mix all of the above together and drizzle this salad with olive oil. Add salt and chilli powder to taste and garnish with fresh basil or parsley.

Bread

Bread goes with braai like brandy goes with coke. There are four types of bread that the real braaier needs to master and they are discussed in this chapter. I love all four of them, but not equally. *Braaibroodjies* were, are and always will be my absolute favourite.

Garlic bread is a fantastic snack when standing around the fire and a great side dish to any meal. Just make it properly, as per the recipe, and don't skimp on the ingredients.

Pot bread and *roosterkoek*, fresh from the fire with butter and jam, goes well with any braaied meal, and making them will also introduce you to the ancient art of baking your own bread. *Roosterkoek* is also the classy and tasty alternative to shop-bought rolls in all the burger recipes.

TRADITIONAL *BRAAIBROODJIES*

The *braaibroodjie* (braaied toasted sandwich) is the highlight of many a braai. Those not yet emancipated by the fact that you don't need meat at every braai, frequently braai meat as a pretext when all they actually want is *braaibroodjies*.

WHAT YOU NEED

(makes 9 *braaibroodjies*)

1 pre-sliced loaf white bread (usually contains at least 18 useable slices)

300 g cheddar cheese (sliced – grate if you want to, but it falls out easier)

1 large onion (sliced into rings)

4 tomatoes, sliced (you need 2 slices per *braaibroodjie* and there are on average 5 useable slices per tomato)

chutney

butter

salt and pepper

WHAT TO DO TO ASSEMBLE

1. Butter all the slices of bread on one side. Slice the cheese, onion and tomatoes.

2. Place half the bread slices butter side down, spread chutney on them and evenly distribute all the cheese, tomato and onion on top. Grind salt and pepper over that. Cover with the remaining bread slices, butter side facing up. Some people try and make an issue out of whether to butter the *braaibroodjie* on the outside or inside. There is no debate; you butter it on the outside. This makes a golden-brown finished product, and also keeps the *braaibroodjie* from sticking to the grid.

WHAT TO DO TO BRAAI

Braaibroodjies are always braaied in a *toeklaprooster* (hinged grid). Using an open grid for this is silly to the point of stupid. You want very gentle heat and you need to turn them often. They are ready when the outsides are golden brown, the cheese has melted and all the other ingredients are properly heated all the way through. If the outsides are burnt before the cheese is melted you've failed.

Many people braai the *broodjies* right at the end, after the meat. The advantage is that the coals are then quite gentle but the disadvantage is that your meat then rests until it is cold.

An alternative trick is to have two identical braai grids. Braai your meat in the bottom one and your *braaibroodjies* in the other, resting right on top of the meat grid. When you want to turn the meat, first remove the top grid with the *braaibroodjies* in it. Turn both grids and then replace, meat grid below, bread grid on top. The heat will reach the bread and start to melt the cheese but the meat will protect the bread from the direct heat and getting burnt. Right at the end, when you remove the meat, give the bread solid direct heat for about a minute on each side to get some colour.

AND . . .

■ If you're having a breakfast braai then fry a few eggs sunny side up in a pan on the braai or stove, and when your *braaibroodjies* are finished gently pull them open and insert one egg into each. You now have a breakfast *braaibroodjie*.

■ In addition to *braaibroodjies*, boerewors rolls are one of the true classics of the South African braai: a fresh piece of braaied boerewors in a hotdog roll. The boerewors *braaibroodjie* gives you the best of both worlds. While braaing your *braaibroodjies*, also braai some thin boerewors on the side. When both are done, gently pull each *braaibroodjie* open and insert a few short pieces of boerewors into them. At the time of writing the book, this was one of my favourite dishes.

ROOSTERKOEK

Baking bread is an ancient skill, and a fulfilling one, so you need to master it. The tricky part is making the dough. If you've never made dough in your life, the recipe below will probably look quite daunting the first time you read it. Take a deep breath, drink a beer, and read it again. Like riding a bicycle it's surprisingly easy once you get the hang of it.

WHAT YOU NEED

(makes 12 decent-sized *roosterkoek*)

1 kg cake flour (as the 'koek' part of the Afrikaans name implies, use cake flour but white bread flour is also fine if that is what's on hand)

10 g instant yeast (Instant yeast comes in 10 g packets, specifically done that way to make it easy, as you need 10 g for every 1 kg of flour. That coincidently is also why this recipe calls for 1 kg of flour and 10 g of yeast.)

1 tot sugar

½ tot salt

lukewarm water in a jug (you'll need roughly just more than 2 cups of water)

2 tots olive oil

WHAT TO DO

1. Sift the flour into a bowl that is at least three times bigger than 1 kg of flour, and preferably even bigger. If you are in the middle of the bush and do not have a sieve on hand then skip the sifting part and just chuck the flour into a big enough bowl. If you only have a 1 kg bag of flour and no more, save a little for step 10.

2. Add the yeast and sugar to the flour (do not add the salt yet) and mix thoroughly with your clean hand.

3. Add the salt and toss around. (Adding the salt directly onto the yeast will kill the yeast.)

4. Add the lukewarm water bit by bit and knead the dough continuously. As soon as there is no dry flour left, you've added enough water. Take care not to add too much water, as this will lead to the dough being runny and falling through the grid. *Roosterkoek* falling through the grid is just no good. For 1 kg of flour you will probably use just more than 2 cups of water.

5. If you think you have enough water in there, add the 2 tots of olive oil.

6. Knead the dough well for about 10 minutes until none of it sticks to your fingers anymore and it forms one big pliable piece.

7. Cover the bowl with a damp kitchen towel or cling wrap and place in a warm area for 10 minutes.

8. Remove the kitchen towel or cling wrap and knead the dough again for a minute or 2.

9. Cover the dough as before and let it rise for at least 30 minutes.

10. Use your recently washed hands to flatten the dough onto a table or plank that is covered in flour and also lightly sprinkle flour on top of the dough. Your aim is to create a rectangular or square piece of dough.

11. Use a sharp knife and cut into squares and let these rise for a few minutes one final time.

12. Gently lay the *roosterkoek* onto the grid with enough space between them for them to rise while they cook. Bake over very gentle coals for about 20 minutes, turning often. A *roosterkoek* is ready when it sounds hollow when you tap on it. Alternatively, insert the blade of your pocketknife or multi-tool into them as a test. If the blade comes out clean the *roosterkoek* is ready.

AND . . .

■ *Roosterkoek* can be served in many ways: my favourites are with boerewors as a boerewors roll; with jam and cheese; or as the roll of a prego roll.

■ Some supermarkets sell fresh dough. If you've bought some of that, start making your *roosterkoek* from step 10.

■ If you've never made dough in your life there is no shame in asking someone who has done it before to show you what it means to 'knead it into one pliable piece'.

POT BREAD

Making the dough for pot bread is slightly easier than making the dough for *roosterkoek* as it's not such an issue if you add a little bit too much water. The bread is baked in a pot and the dough is going nowhere, unlike a runny *roosterkoek* that will sink through the grid. Baking bread in a pot comes at a price though as you cannot see what is going on so burning the bread is a greater risk.

WHAT YOU NEED

(feeds roughly 12)

1 kg white bread flour (or cake flour if that is what's on hand)

10 g instant yeast (Instant yeast comes in 10 g packets, specifically done that way to make it easy, as you need 10 g for every 1 kg of flour. That coincidently is also why this recipe calls for 1 kg of flour and 10 g of yeast.)

1 tot sugar

½ tot salt

lukewarm water in a jug (you'll need roughly just more than 2 cups of water)

2 tots olive oil

butter

WHAT TO DO

1. Sift the flour into a bowl that is at least three times bigger than 1 kg of flour, but preferably even bigger. If you are in the middle of the bush and do not have a sieve on hand then skip the sifting part and just chuck the flour into a big enough bowl.

2. Add the yeast and sugar to the flour (do not add the salt yet) and mix thoroughly with clean hands.

3. Add the salt and toss around. (Adding salt directly onto yeast will kill the yeast.)

4. Add the lukewarm water bit by bit and knead the dough continuously. When there is no dry flour left, you've added enough water. For 1 kg of flour you will probably use about 2½ cups of water.

5. Once you have enough water in there, add the 2 tots of olive oil.

6. Knead the dough properly for about 10 minutes until none of it sticks to your fingers anymore and it forms one big pliable piece. If this simply never happens, you added too much water. Add more flour to fix it.

7. Cover the bowl with a damp kitchen towel or cling wrap and place in a warm area for 10 minutes. During this time you need to smear the inside of the pot and bottom of the lid really well with butter.

8. Remove the kitchen towel or cling wrap and knead the dough again for a minute or two. Now put the dough into the pot. There needs to be space for the bread to rise when the lid is on.

If there isn't enough space, the pot is too small. Remove some of the dough and bake *roosterkoek* with it.

9. Place the pot in a warm area and let the bread rise in the pot for 30 minutes.

10. Now you need to bake the pot bread in even heat for about 1 hour. Even heat means all parts of the pot, and bread, need to be equally exposed to the heat. If there is a very hot fire nearby you need to turn the pot regularly. Place the pot on coals and also place coals on the lid. As the coals below or on top of the pot start to cool off, replace them with new ones. Never add too much heat, or it will burn. I usually take it quite easy on the heat when baking pot bread for fear of burning the thing but it's entirely possible your bread will be ready in 40 minutes; you will have to check.

11. A pot bread is ready when it sounds hollow when you tap on it (you'll need to remove the lid to do this). Then insert the blade of a pocketknife into it as the final test. If the blade comes out clean the pot bread is ready.

AND . . .

Sometimes you burn a pot bread. It's just one of those unfortunate facts of life. If you don't, give yourself a pat on the back. If you do, just cut away the burnt part and adjust your technique slightly next time.

GARLIC BREAD

What an extraordinary meal. Works very well as a snack around the fire and fits equally well as a side dish to any braaied food. There's a reason why home-made garlic bread tastes better than the ones you buy in the super-market: when you make your own garlic bread, you use a fresh ba-guette that you bought that day. When you buy ready-made garlic bread at the store, who knows how stale that bread might be?

WHAT YOU NEED (feeds 4–6)

1 baguette (French loaf)
½ cup salted butter (soft)
5 cloves garlic (crushed or chopped)
1 tot fresh parsley (chopped)
½ tot lemon juice
1 tsp pepper
a roll of tinfoil

WHAT TO DO

1. If the baguette is very long, make two shorter garlic breads.

2. Slice the baguette into 2 cm thick slices, but keep those slices in order. Your ability to keep those slices in the right order is one of the distinguishing factors between good and awesome garlic bread.

3. Heat the butter slightly so that it's nice and soft. Now mix the butter, garlic, parsley, lemon juice and pepper together.

4. Keeping the bread slices in order, place them on a piece of tinfoil that is large enough to wrap the whole bread in. Always place the bread on the foil before you butter it. Any butter you spill will be wrapped up in the foil and be absorbed by the bread.

5. Spread the butter onto one side of each slice and replace them on the foil in order. Make sure the butter goes right to the edges of each slice. On the finished product, another distinguish-ing factor in garlic bread quality is whether the edges of each slice are dry or whether they were properly buttered.

6. If there is any leftover butter, spread it over the top of the bread.

7. Wrap the garlic bread tightly in foil and braai for 12 minutes over high heat, turning to expose all sides to the heat. As the bread is tightly wrapped in foil and will not absorb all that much flavour from the braai, you may also prefer to bake it in an oven on 180°C for 12 minutes.

AND . . .

If you want to make the garlic bread business class, also mix some grated cheddar into the butter. If you want to make it first class, mix grated Parmesan cheese into the butter. If you want to make it fighter plane, mix in a chopped chilli.

Salads

The publisher felt that as this is a braai book I should not include any salad recipes, but I disagreed. There are three salads I really think you should learn to produce and ought to serve at your braais, and their recipes follow here.

In my opinion, this makes the book more complete; and your ability to make three salads properly makes you a better braaier, and person. So depending on whether you like the salads being here or not, you now know whom to address your letters of complaint to.

The chicken Caesar salad on page 88 is more of a meal than a salad and so even the publisher is happy with that one.

POTATO SALAD

This potato salad is pretty gourmet; if you're going to eat salad you might as well make it properly. The photo on the opposite page shows the radish slices with the green bits still on but you have to cut them off when making the salad. The food stylist, Brita du Plessis, insisted I leave them on for the photo; she reckoned it looks nicer.

WHAT YOU NEED (feeds 6–8)

1 kg potatoes
1 medium-sized onion (chopped)
1 tot cider vinegar
½ tot mustard
½ cup mayonnaise
½ cup plain white yoghurt
(I like the Greek type)
salt and ground black pepper
fresh parsley (chopped)

Include some or all of the following optional extras to make the salad taste extra good:

300 g smoked ham (cut into blocks)
3 tots pickled gherkin (chopped)
3 radishes
(washed, trimmed and finely chopped)
3 hard-boiled eggs
(peeled and roughly chopped)

WHAT TO DO

1. Wash and then cook the potatoes a few hours before or even the previous day, and let them cool down. (Peeling them is entirely optional; I think the skins give them more taste.) Potatoes are ready when the skins start to burst and you can press a fork into them. This usually happens after about 20 minutes in boiling water. Although not a crisis, try not to overcook them; we are not making mash.

2. If you are going to add them to the salad, cut the ham, gherkins, radishes and hard-boiled eggs and set aside.

3. Slice the potatoes and mix with the chopped onion.

4. Heat the vinegar and mustard in a pan and pour over the potato slices, stir and then let it rest for a few minutes.

5. Now add the mayonnaise, yoghurt, salt and pepper, and your choice of gherkin, egg, radish and ham. Also add some liquid from the pickled gherkin jar but not so much that the leftover gherkins in the jar will dry out. Toss well, cover and let the salad rest in the fridge for at least 30 minutes before serving.

6. Garnish with chopped parsley.

AND . . .

■ Remember, if you use fat-free, tasteless mayonnaise and yoghurt, you will have fat-free, tasteless potato salad.
■ If you like sweeter potato salad, replace some, or all, of the half cup of plain yoghurt with condensed milk.

CURRY PASTA SALAD

This is one of those dishes where the reward in taste completely outweighs the incredibly easy process of making it. It goes very well with absolutely any braaied meat or fish.

WHAT YOU NEED

(feeds 6–8 as a side dish)

250 g pasta

1 × 420 g tin of sliced peaches

1 cup mayonnaise

1 cup plain yoghurt

1 tot curry powder

1 tsp salt

just less than 1 tsp black pepper

1 red apple (a sweet variety)

1 tot lemon juice

½ onion

1 pepper (green, yellow or red)

WHAT TO DO

1. Boil the pasta according to the instructions on the packaging. When it's done, drain it and rinse under cold water to cool it down and shock it out of cooking any more.

2. Open the tin of peaches and pour the syrup into a bowl with the mayonnaise and yoghurt. Mix these three with the curry powder, salt and black pepper.

3. Core the apple and then chop it into cubes (peeling is optional). Immediately toss the lemon juice over the apple pieces to stop them going brown and then mix that into the curry sauce.

4. Chop the onion, pepper and peach slices into cubes and mix into the curry sauce.

5. Mix the sauce with the pasta and refrigerate for at least 30 minutes before serving. As with most curries the flavours develop with time and chances are you will like the taste even more the next day.

GREEK SALAD

You've got to know the rules to break them. Here is the immortal Greek salad recipe. Once you've mastered it, progress by also adding fresh basil leaves but re-member that a Greek salad never contains lettuce. Never.

WHAT YOU NEED (feeds 6–8)

5 large tomatoes
(or lots of cherry tomatoes)

1 cucumber

1 pepper (green, yellow or red)

1 large red onion

200 g feta cheese
(200 g is one small container, drained)

1-2 cups black olives (pitted)

2 tots olive oil

1 tot lemon juice

1 tot mix of chopped fresh oregano and parsley

1 tsp salt

1 tsp pepper

1 tsp sugar

WHAT TO DO

1. Wash the tomatoes, cucumber and pepper and slice into blocks.

2. Slice the onion into thin rings and mix it with the above. In a Greek salad the tomatoes, cucumber and pepper should be in blocks but the onion in rings.

3. Remove the pits from the olives and cut the feta into blocks. Mix into the salad.

4. Make the dressing by mixing together the oil, lemon juice, oregano, parsley, salt, pepper and sugar. Pour this over the salad and toss well.

AND . . .

As with all recipes, the quality of the ingredients is vitally important. The Dutch have a word for those rose-tinted green and white tomatoes that taste like nothing: water bombs. Make sure you buy red tomatoes that taste like tomato.

Desserts

Yes, desserts, prepared on the braai. If you've read the book this far you should know that I'm not going to waste your precious time and that these will be worthwhile trying.

And read the note in the braaied marshmallow recipe on page 194 and use the opportunity to initiate your children into the art of braaing – you can't start too early.

BRAAIED BANANA AND CARAMELISED PINEAPPLE

Braaied banana and caramelised pineapple with ice-cream and golden syrup is every bit as good as it looks on paper.

WHAT YOU NEED (feeds 6)

1 pineapple
6 bananas
sugar (brown or white)
ice-cream (or cream or crème fraîche)
golden syrup

WHAT TO DO

1. Peel the pineapple and cut into six slices of even thickness. Coat both sides of each pineapple slice in sugar by either dipping it in sugar or sprinkling sugar over both sides. The bananas are braaied as is, unpeeled and in their skins.

2. Braai the pineapple slices and bananas over medium coals. The bananas are ready when they are completely black all over, and the pineapple is ready when the sugar on both sides has caramelised.

3. Remove from the fire and slice deep into the bananas along the inside curve. Open up the bananas by pressing simultaneously on both ends. Each banana should now look like an Indian canoe (paddle boat).

4. Put one banana and pineapple slice in each dessert bowl and place a scoop of ice-cream into each banana. Cream or crème fraîche also works. Drizzle golden syrup or honey over the contents of each bowl and serve immediately.

ICE-CREAM WITH FRESHLY MADE CARAMEL SAUCE

If for whatever reason you'll have a braai fire burning for a few hours anyhow, this is a delicious dessert that you should prepare.

WHAT YOU NEED (feeds 6)

1 tin condensed milk
ice-cream
a cast-iron pot and water

WHAT TO DO

1. Remove all labels from the tin and use a can-opener to pierce two small holes in the lid of the tin, on opposite sides of the lid. A bit of condensed milk might escape from these holes but don't worry about that.

2. Position the tin upright in the cast-iron pot, and pour water into the pot to a level just below the lid.

3. Place the pot on the fire and bring the water to the boil. The water needs to boil for the next 3½ hours. You need to monitor the pot constantly as the water evaporates and you need to keep topping it up. Depending on how tightly your lid closes, you might need to refill it a few times. If the pot runs dry the can will explode. My mother tells a great story about an unexpected guest, an exploding can and a kitchen ceiling covered in caramel. If you ever meet her, ask her about it.

4. During the process a bit of the condensed milk might end up in the water and make the water boil foamy and white. Don't worry about that. If the rapidly boiling water seems to cover your tin and seems to be going in the holes, don't worry, it doesn't. All you need to worry about is that the pot never runs dry.

5. After 3½ hours remove the can from the pot using tongs. Wipe the excess water from the tin. As soon as you want to, cut open the can and gently stir the caramel with a teaspoon until it is smooth.

6. Pour or scoop the caramel over bowls of ice-cream and serve immediately.

AND . . .

Go nuts! You can make the above recipe even more awesome by topping it with some toasted nuts. Roughly chop a few pecan nuts and fry them in a dry pan for about a minute. The moment they start to brown and release flavour they are ready.

FLAMBÉED PEACHES

This dish looks impressive yet preparing it is incredibly easy.

WHAT YOU NEED (feeds 3-4)
1 x 420 g tin peach slices
a couple of tots brandy
vanilla ice-cream (or cream or custard)

WHAT TO DO

1. Open the tin and pour the peaches and syrup into a fireproof pan.

2. Position the pan over flames or coals. Stand the pan evenly so its ingredients don't spill.

3. Bring to the boil and let it simmer until the sauce starts to thicken. Now pour a generous dash of brandy into the pan and tip the pan towards the flames, setting the contents alight.

4. As soon as the flames have died down, the dessert is ready to serve with ice-cream, cream or custard.

AND . . .

- If you are making this recipe for many people and use more than one tin of peaches, don't add the sauce from all the tins to the pan. The sauce gets a bit too much and will take a very long time to reduce and thicken.
- When served with long-life custard or evaporated milk, this is a perfect recipe for a camping trip in the bush or on a deserted beach.

MARSHMALLOWS IN BAR-ONE SAUCE

There is a certain age at which your toddler isn't quite ready to take charge of the lamb shank *potjie*. This recipe is a perfect opportunity to get him or her started in the basics of making a great dish in a cast-iron pot on the fire.

WHAT YOU NEED

1 big pack of marshmallows

3 Bar-One chocolates

3 tots cream or cold milk

bamboo skewers
(or any sticks from the veld)

WHAT TO DO

1. Add the cream and chocolates to a medium-to-small cast-iron pot and place the pot over medium heat.

2. As the pot heats up, the cream and chocolate should heat up together and the chocolate will melt. Stir continuously until you have smooth chocolate sauce.

3. Remove the pot from the fire. As the pot is made from cast iron it will keep its heat and the chocolate sauce will stay warm for a while.

4. Put marshmallows on skewers, dip them in the chocolate sauce and enjoy.

AND . . .

Encourage your kids to braai some of the skewered marshmallows by holding the skewer over the flames or coals. Braaing marshmallows will teach your kids the fundamental principles of braaing chicken: gentle heat and turn often; a skin that can easily burn before the inside is done.

WHAT IS A MAN-OVEN?

Man-Oven is my collective term for those outdoor cooking devices that are powered by charcoal or briquette fires, where you mostly cook with indirect heat, and where the food is usually baked with the lid closed. You typically use a Man-Oven to braai larger cuts of meat.

Some Man-Ovens are powered by gas but if you want to read more about them you will have to buy a different book. The best-known Man-Ovens in South Africa are the kettle braai-type made by brands like Weber, Cadac and Bushbaby.

At the time of writing this book the superior Kamado-style grills made from ceramic were starting to penetrate the South African market. A Kamado-style grill is best powered by the more natural charcoal (as opposed to briquettes) and, thanks to its ceramic shell, it has high efficiency, excellent insulation and the ability to accurately hold very high and very low temperatures for a prolonged period of time. Why would you need to accurately hold low temperatures for prolonged periods of time? To braai non-traditional cuts like pork shoulder (and make pulled pork) or brisket, of course. These things are beyond the scope of this book but incredibly simple to prepare in a Kamado-style Man-Oven. It seals properly which results in moister food. The efficient venting system and good insulation of a Kamado oven permits precise temperature control and allows you to perfect the successful braaing of all large cuts of meat.

During some of my travels I was fortunate enough to meet the inventor and owner of premier German Kamado oven producer, Monolith. He helped me to import one to South Africa and for the past few years I have used it at home to bake chickens and pork bellies or smoke fish on the days that I don't braai in the traditional sense of the word. On days you don't feel like meat, put the pizza stone in your Kamado oven and with the intense heat and fire you can bake extra thin-based pizzas to rival the best restaurants. At the time of writing you could already buy Monolith braais in South Africa. Google it.

When cooking large pieces of meat in a Man-Oven you do it over indirect heat. In a Kamado oven like my Monolith it means inserting the deflector plate that comes with the unit. In a kettle braai like a Weber it means making two heaps of coals on the sides of the bottom grid and placing the meat right in the middle of the top grid. After an hour a kettle braai usually starts to lose heat so you will need to top up the coals. A Kamado braai will keep going until whatever you need to cook is done on one fill.

AND FINALLY ...

ACKNOWLEDGEMENTS

If you're still reading the book and made it all the way to the back, thanks! I hope you found it useful.

- Thanks to my family: Deetje, Jan, Marietjie, Jack, Ina Mari, Christina, Kennet, Marlies and Claas for assisting me during many years of 'tough research', also known as 'braaing'.

- If you've ever braaied with me, you helped with this book. In particular thanks to my friends (and their fathers) who braaied with me over the years in Stellenbosch, Blouberg, De Fonteine, Matjiesvlei and in Decembers along the Garden Route. Special mention to Ernst and Adele for performing the tough task of braaing non-stop for more than a month during the final stages of completing this book to see whether the recipes made sense when read and performed by an objective person.

- Food stylist Brita du Plessis and photographer Matthys van Lill never gave up until every photo was perfect – much respect! Nicky and Leigh, thanks for the coffee, tea and everything else.

- Louise from Bookstorm who contacted me two years ago, asked whether I would like to write a book, and then waited patiently for two years while I did that.

- To my mentor and friend Michiel, thank you for everything.

FINAL THOUGHTS

- Never be afraid or embarrassed to ask the butcher for advice or assistance. Their job is to provide you with service.

- Not everybody likes equal amounts of salt in their food. When in doubt, add less salt when you prepare the meal and make one firm and clear statement to all guests when seated that salt is provided at the table, as the food might need more of it.

- Always make sure you have enough good coals. The easiest and most enjoyable way to ensure this is to have a stockpile of dry braai wood on hand and starting a large fire with it.

- When in doubt always under-braai meat. You can easily return it to the fire if it's still a bit raw but once you over-braai meat and it is dry, there is no way to reverse the process.

- These days men don't need to be the hunters they were 100 years ago and catching your own fish is also not seen as the requisite skill it used to be. But you do need to be able to make the perfect braai. It's one of those things that should be done without any fuss and minimal fanfare. Actions and results should speak louder than words and there should be a clear demonstration that you have deep and thorough knowledge of the intricacies that surround this ancient and primitive art. It's just one of those things that separates the men from the boys.

First edition, first impression 2012

Published jointly by
Bookstorm (Pty) Limited and Pan Macmillan South Africa
Suite 10   Private Bag X19
Private Bag X12   Northlands 2116
Cresta 2118   Johannesburg
Johannesburg   South Africa
South Africa   www.panmacmillan.co.za
www.bookstorm.co.za

Distributed by Pan Macmillan
via Booksite Afrika

Edited by Pat Botes
Proofread by Pat Botes
Food stylist Brita du Plessis
Photography by Matthys van Lill
Cover design by Jaco Erasmus
Printed by Ultra Litho (Pty) Ltd,
Johannesburg

INDEX

The Jan Braai Rules

1. Nothing beats a real wood fire.

2. Gas is Afrikaans for a guest at your braai, not something you braai with.

3. Braaing is the only fat-negative way of cooking food. Even when you steam food, the fat in it stays behind. When you braai, the fat drips out. Be healthy and braai your food.

4. Try never to braai with indigenous wood. Alien vegetation like Rooikrans and black wattle drink lots of groundwater so rather burn them. Besides, after all these sports world cups they've knocked us out of, it feels good to burn Australian rubbish.

5. Braaing is a direct form of energy use, from the coals to your meat. With conventional electricity there is a lot spillage between the power plant, power lines, electricity box, wires, stove and pan. If you love the earth, braai.

6. Have enough ice at your braai. Use it for your Klippies and coke, to keep beer cold, and to treat burn wounds with.

7. Smoke flies to pretty people, so have enough of them at your braai and there will be no smoke in your eyes.

8. Animals eat grass, leaves and vegetables all their lives and convert it to meat. Eating meat is like eating vitamin pills.

9. A cow must only be killed once. Do not braai you steak until the flavour is dead.

10. A *braaibroodjie* is your chance in life to have your bread buttered on both sides – use it.